Praise for *The Dynar*

I'm a big Shelley fan. Anyone who knows Shelley personally will tell you she is refreshingly open and honest in her relationships, and she has carried this over into her book, sharing with her readers the often raw truth of her own leadership journey, even when it was confronting for her to do so. …For the new leader just starting their journey or for those looking to re-energise their leadership style, Shelley has something for everyone in this simple no-nonsense book.

Anne Young, Head of Australia Operations, ANZ

Shelley Flett is a rising star in the field of helping leaders and their teams excel. *The Dynamic Leader* is a how-to-guide to the basics of leading – but don't think it's a book only for the less experienced leader; quite the opposite. It's a universal truth. The basics are the hardest thing to consistently adhere to, even if you've achieved success. This book will provide a handy compass back to what really matters.

Darren Hill, Executive Director, Pragmatic Thinking

The Dynamic Leader is written in simple language that anyone can understand, and that is the beauty of Shelley's work. She calls it 'Uncomplicated Leadership' – learning the basics of communication, engagement and team leadership, that will help any emerging or established leader create high-performing teams. I enjoyed reading Shelley's book and highly recommend it to anyone who needs to improve their team dynamic.

Alma Besserdin, FCPHR, MAICD, Founder and Director
Wimmigrants Pty Ltd

This book is designed to help everyday managers transition into leadership roles. It recognises that being a new manager can be a challenging, tough and often lonely path. It addresses the reality that being a manager is no longer about you as an individual contributor but about your ability to deliver results through others while helping them learn, grow and perform. It is about investing in relationships, inspiring respect, building capability and growing future leaders.

This book is about helping managers to transition to become dynamic leaders...someone that everyone wants to follow.

Narelle Burke, Global Head of Talent & Leadership Development, Kantar

The odds are when your leadership isn't getting you the outcomes you desire the problem is with you not the team. *The Dynamic Leader* is a great balance of theory and practical advice pitched at the right level that you can implement quickly. This is a refreshingly honest book about looking in the mirror.

Suzanne Wood, State General Manager, Mortgage Broker Distribution VIC/TAS, Westpac

The Dynamic Leader is an insightful and easy read, with many practical tips you can apply straight away. I have read a lot of leadership books and there simply isn't one like this! It's such a refreshingly raw and honest capture from Shelley of all things leadership: the good, bad and ugly. Shelley explains just how you can be a kick-arse dynamic leader! I loved the messages throughout about being your true self, allowing yourself to be human and showing vulnerability, that it's okay to be friends with your team and how to balance your focus on people and results. This is a must-read for new and experienced leaders alike. There are so many people I can't wait to share it with!

Brylie Gorman, Team Manager - Business Specialists, Performance and Innovation, TAC

The Dynamic Leader is an exceptional book written in a manner that will not only resonate with leaders, but with parents, friends, family members and anyone dealing with people. It highlights the importance of building strong relationships through trust, authenticity and doing what's right to achieve success. *The Dynamic Leader* model makes the complex simple and provides tips to engage and influence others to achieve their goals... A great read for anyone serious about making an impact on others.

Islam Hassan, Head of Growth, Westpac

Shelley's book presents a fantastic nine-stage model that engages and clarifies for leaders how they can be a positive influence with imperative self-awareness. It's a fantastic resource to assist any leader to remain focused, provide a different perspective and importantly it offers practical application.

Justine Teggelove, CEO, Rodine

Shelley Flett is the first business and leadership coach that I gravitate to when I want to assist my leaders in their development. Through her vast experience in helping countless leaders and organisations through the journey of true leadership, Shelley has been able to write a book that takes you on a journey of realisation, of how much can be achieved by applying the three key elements in a dynamic leader, investing in relationships, inspiring respect and influencing results. If you have a desire to cultivate your leadership skills to become a dynamic leader then I encourage you: don't walk to meet Shelley Flett, run!

Spiz Constandinou, Head of Practice Support, MYOB

Shelley has amazing passion, energy and commitment in everything she does, both personally and professionally. She is a truly inspirational leader, and throughout this book you will discover the vulnerability and authenticity of her own leadership journey. Shelley's character and personality come through on every page as she shares her own experiences and stories, intertwined with simple and effective leadership concepts and competencies to provide a compelling reason for becoming a dynamic leader. So whether you are moving into your first leadership role or you are an experienced leader wanting to become a more effective and dynamic leader this is a book I would highly recommend you read, put into practice and share with others.

Barry Edgar, GAICD, Head of Business Initiatives, Business Enablement & Growth, Consumer Banking & Wealth, NAB

It's hard to think of a time in history when the world has been changing more rapidly than now. The leadership challenges that exist today are not always a good guide to those that leaders will face in the near future. That is why *The Dynamic Leader* is an essential companion for new and experienced leaders as they make the transition on what is sometimes a lonely road in these changing times. Using real-life examples, Shelley Flett reveals where, how and when to shift your focus towards becoming a dynamic leader that others will be inspired to follow.

Matthew Hocking, Lawyer and Senior Executive

Every leader, whether new or seasoned, needs to have this book in their tool kit. Leadership principles can be overly theoretical and dry, however Shelley's conversational and humorous style makes this book a delightfully compelling read, where her use of real-life examples brings the theory to life. She has a gift for making concepts highly practical and easy to apply. Every chapter is filled with nuggets of gold. Implement any one of them and I guarantee your leadership effectiveness will increase.

Shelley, you are the student who has become the master. I am and will always be your biggest fan. With love and gratitude Mei.

Mei Ouw, Leadership Development & Executive Coach, Mei Ouw Consulting

Shelley is one of the most authentic, down to earth, warts-and-all storytellers that you could have the privilege to meet. She leads from the heart and from the front taking us through nine practical steps that underpin leadership in managing tasks and people.

The Dynamic Leader is a great read that busts myths along the way, while arming you with strategies and tactics to 'become the leader that others are inspired to follow'.

Fiona Keough, CEO, Auscontact Association

THE DYNAMIC LEADER

Become the leader others
are inspired to follow

SHELLEY FLETT

First published in 2019 by Major Street Publishing Pty Ltd
PO Box 106, Highett, Vic. 3190
E: info@majorstreet.com.au
W: majorstreet.com.au
M: +61 421 707 983

Quantity sales. Special discounts are available on quantity purchases by corporations, associations and others. For details, contact Lesley Williams using the contact details above.

Individual sales. Major Street publications are available through most bookstores. They can also be ordered directly from Major Street's online bookstore at www.majorstreet.com.au.

Orders for university textbook/course adoption use. For orders of this nature, please contact Lesley Williams using the contact details above.

NATIONAL LIBRARY OF AUSTRALIA

A catalogue record for this book is available from the National Library of Australia

ISBN: 978-0-6484795-0-5

Internal design by Production Works
Cover design by Simone Geary
Photo by Simon Heenan, owner of SimonLiveFree and founder of Melbourne Made
Printed in Australia by Ovato, an Accredited ISO AS/NZS 14001:2004 Environmental Management System Printer.

10 9 8 7 6 5 4 3 2 1

This book is dedicated to my big sis, Narelle. Without your guidance and feedback, I would never have learnt the lessons of being a true leader!

Huge thanks also to my husband, my rock, Marcell, for his unwavering support and encouragement.

CONTENTS

ABOUT THE AUTHOR

Shelley Flett grew up on a farm in country Victoria with her parents and three siblings. She learnt to work hard and to never expect anything for nothing – when there was a job to be done, everyone rolled their sleeves up and got on with it, no questions asked. At school Shelley really struggled with the way she was taught, finding theory and content difficult to absorb in the absence of context and real-life examples. She never understood how letters translated in mathematical equations, such as 2(x + 8y), or what the difference was between a noun and a verb (or why it even mattered). She rarely asked questions because the text book responses she received still didn't make sense, and so she quickly formed the belief she was 'dumb'.

Shelley lowered her expectations of what life after school would look like and secured her first full-time role in the local cheese factory, figuring she would work her way up over time. What she discovered was her ability to learn and pick things up quickly – once she understood the 'why' and the context in which processes and theory were applied. So, while Shelley never went to university, she developed a hunger to learn and opted for TAFE and other short courses that included a high amount of experiential learning and context over theory and content.

Now, as a speaker, facilitator, trainer and coach, Shelley has developed a reputation for her simplicity and ability to teach in a basic, uncomplicated way. She uses plain language and provides context, case studies and interactive discussion to ensure participants can apply their lessons back in the workplace. Her approach is simple but very effective.

Shelley is a Master Practitioner in Neuro Linguistic Programming (NLP), holds a Diploma of Leadership Coaching and Mentoring, a Cert IV in Business & Personal Coaching and a Diploma of Business Management. She is DiSC, Values Pendulum and Green Belt Six Sigma accredited and is also an accredited coach through the International Coaching Federation (ICF).

She lives in the south eastern suburbs of Melbourne with her three children, Luis, Riley and Eva and her South African–born husband, Marcell. They have a ritual where they eat dinner every night at the table, with a no-electronics policy during this time to ensure they are completely present. Shelley isn't that interested in material possessions but more in having fun – while her lifestyle may appear modest, it's full of adventure and excitement and she wouldn't trade it for the world. Her happy places include riding her motorbike, snow skiing with Marcell, visiting wineries and getting outside with her kids.

INTRODUCTION

This book focuses on helping you become a dynamic leader – the kind of leader who others will aspire to follow. The kind of leader I wish I had had to follow.

I write this book as a leader who got it terribly wrong before getting it wonderfully right. Throughout the book, I share with you my experiences and the journey I took as I moved from one extreme of leadership to the other. Most importantly, I share the incredibly tough lessons I learnt along the way. These are the lessons I applied to my own team while working in banking, and have since developed into a one-day Dynamic Leaders program I run with new and emerging leaders from a wide variety of organisations. The feedback I've received from this program is that leaders leave with a new perspective on how to approach leadership, and feel more aware of how they prefer to lead along with what others expect. They learn to say what needs to be said, do what needs to be done and be the leader their staff aspire to be.

My leadership journey

My definition of a leader in my early 20s was someone who told others what to do and made sure things were running as they should. I honestly didn't think they did much of the work themselves – at least, that's what I'd observed in the leaders I'd worked under. This definition was further enforced when I first became manager of a bar in a pub in Surrey, United Kingdom (during a three-year backpacking adventure across the world). My role was to make sure the staff were working, the rosters were up-to-date and the clients were happy. It was also my responsibility to drink with the clients and make sure they were enjoying themselves – best job ever, right! In the beginning, it was a lot of fun and my tolerance for alcohol became exceptional but I wasn't very liked by the staff, who worked pretty hard, and the shine wore off pretty quickly. After six months of a fairly permanent alcohol-induced-state, I moved on.

My next experience as a leader occurred after I'd returned to Australia and was working in a contact centre. I started as a customer service consultant and was quickly promoted into the role of senior officer and then team leader. When I became the senior officer, my team leader suggested I cut the friendship ties with my peers and 'draw a line' between them and me. My leader was concerned that if I maintained the relationship I had with them, I'd open myself up to being taken advantage of and wouldn't gain the respect required for my new position. Not knowing any better and eager to impress, I took the advice and went from being 'fun, friendly Shelley' to 'serious boss Shelley'.

Because of my desire to succeed and eagerness to please, I probably took this advice too literally. I stopped asking people how they were doing and started interrogating them for not meeting targets. When they called in sick, I never asked if they were okay and always assumed they were faking it. Of course, unplanned absences in a contact centre environment are actually higher than in many other industries because of the nature and intensity of the work – in one contact centre where I worked it wasn't unreasonable to answer 100+ calls a day. However, sometimes these 'unplanned' absences did start to seem a little more planned. I remember one particular direct report who, when their sick leave balance would renew (on their yearly anniversary), would take one day of sick leave per week until their leave balance was reduced to zero. They would then work without an absence until the next year's balance renewed. Sure, you might say this was coincidental, but it would happen each year and similar patterns were observed with staff across the team. And in 'serious boss' mode, I became suspicious of everyone's motives.

Similar to many other contact centre leaders, I also became jaded after a while. I took absences personally and felt like my team were conspiring to prevent me from achieving my own targets. To prove a point, although I'm sure no-one noticed, I refused to take any sick leave – even when I should have. I occasionally would leave early but would rarely take a day off, and instead would come into the office coughing all over the place. I'm not sure I proved any point and the result was leaving the organisation after ten years with a balance of almost 3,000 hours of accumulated sick leave.

Some staff responded well to my style of leadership; others, however, were completely put off and their performance deteriorated until they either left the team or left the organisation. I was always able to explain these exits away to my managers (and to myself) as being due to poor performance with a lack of engagement or due to those people not being the right fit to begin with. I never stopped to consider that part of the problem might be me. Feedback on my approach and style of leadership was never given (or, at least, I never heard it), and I was always rated really well for achieving goals and seen as a high performer in my broader team and across the organisation.

When I was promoted to a team leader my behaviour only amplified – having been promoted, I considered myself to be on the right track so didn't see any need to change. My team thought very differently. I remember participating in a 360-degree feedback assessment and taking the responses from my team on my leadership style – where they outlined what they felt I was doing wrong – really badly. Rather than accepting the comments as opportunities to learn, I tried to figure out who had made them so I could justify (and negate) the feedback with my own commentary about the person and why they would have said what they did.

In other words, I took the feedback as a personal attack. Instead of it improving how I led my team, I became very guarded around them. Rather than allowing myself to be vulnerable and open to a learning opportunity, I closed down and considered the people in my team as disposable assets. (Gosh! I actually feel a little embarrassed writing this, but I'm committed to giving you the whole-ugly-truth.) At the time, I believed that my staff were being paid to do a job and if they couldn't do the job, they'd have to look elsewhere because there was no room for people who weren't going to 'pull their weight'.

To be fair, the contact centre environment is a high pressure one and becoming a little frustrated when things aren't going to plan is easy. I was constantly putting out fires and managing personnel issues. Hiring and firing were frequent and it became almost impossible to see the bigger picture – I was up to my eyeballs in drama and it never stopped!

I think my experience of transiting into leadership is something a lot of first-time leaders can relate to. Most will approach their role with a 'task' focused approach. Others will think a 'people' focused approach is more important.

Being task-focused in your leadership approach means your interest is around delivering results, getting things done and/or getting things right. You're focused on process, productivity, efficiency, performance and achievement.

In contrast, a people-focused leadership approach means your interest is around building relationships, getting to know people and ensuring they feel valued. It is around engagement, collaboration, fun, health and personal fulfilment.

And while both approaches have their unique benefits they also have their disadvantages.

Getting the most out of this book

This book guides you towards finding a balance between task and people in your leadership role, and treating both with equal importance. The importance of getting this balance right is what led to me developing my nine-stage Dynamic Leadership model, which I outline in much greater detail in parts II and III of this book. The model is simple to relate to and incorporates all of the interpersonal elements required to succeed as a new leader. Importantly, it helps you focus on the three main elements of leadership: relationships, respect and results.

The model also includes an overarching theme of communication, to help leaders deliver better messages, both verbally and non-verbally, in all interactions with their staff. And it includes an underpinning theme of time, to assist leaders with prioritisation and focusing on the things that matter over the things that come easiest.

Successfully transitioning into leadership requires an element of focus and careful consideration about how you spend your time. Many leaders fall into the trap of 'looking busy' from day one. Rather than sitting back and observing how to best structure their day and time, they jump straight into whatever 'fire' seems to need their attention most.

Or they find whatever they can to make themselves look busy. The approach I offer, through my Dynamic Leadership model, is to embrace your discomfort around not 'doing' and realise the importance of building relationships, listening to your staff and inspiring respect, and influencing results over demanding them.

The following figure shows the model in its entirety. In the chapters in parts II and III, I break the model down and outline each of its main elements.

The Dynamic Leadership model

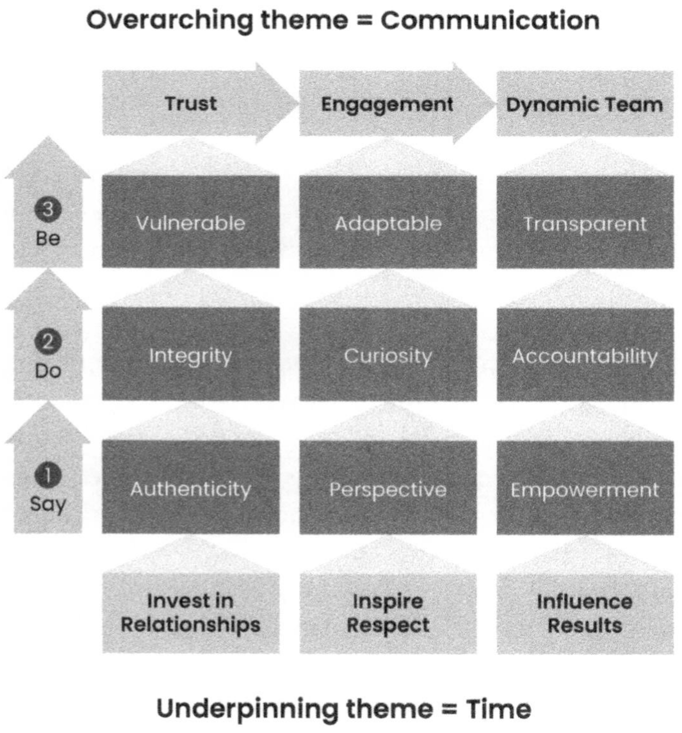

I designed this nine-stage model to help new leaders establish focus and rhythm and become influential. As well as using it myself in my corporate career, I have used it when training leaders over a number of years, refining and adjusting the model over time. This refinement has produced a powerful tool and guidebook leaders can use when they initially enter leadership and continually return to when they're feeling overwhelmed and out of control.

The three core components that result in becoming a dynamic leader – that is, investing in relationships, inspiring respect and influencing results – are not rocket science and are quite simple to comprehend. The model provides an opportunity to uncover blind spots and build awareness around the things that might be holding you back.

This book is for new leaders and also those who may not have had a very positive transition to leadership, and perhaps still feel like they're not a leader worthy of following. It provides the opportunity to focus on the areas that make a difference in a simple, uncomplicated and easy to adopt way, and gives an alternative to the conventional 'command and control' approach to leadership. Ultimately, this book helps set you up for success in a sustainable way. Through investing in relationships, inspiring respect and influencing results, you work smart and your role becomes one of support, guidance and building capability – and of nurturing our future leaders.

By the end of the book, you should have a clear idea of how to become a dynamic leader, and can start putting some of the lessons you've learned into practice. This is your guide book, your travel mate, your 'go-to' place when you feel out of control and need a different perspective. By no means is this book the only thing you'll need to become an amazing leader but it's a great place to start.

One last point: while the book provides a logical and sequential perspective on how I view leadership, I get that you might not have the time or perhaps the patience to read the book from cover to cover. So feel free to skip to the sections that relate to you or, even better, engage me to run the program in your organisation and then use this book as a reference afterwards.

Whatever your planned approach, let's get started!

PART I
THE TRANSITION TO LEADERSHIP

I think one of the hardest things to deal with when transitioning into a leadership role is the loneliness that comes with it. Suddenly you are bound by confidentiality and needing to keep things to yourself, where perhaps in the past you were able to talk issues and challenges through with a colleague. Your peers are just as busy as you so finding time to share thoughts and just hang out are also reduced. Your own manager is busy dealing with their own challenges and sometimes you might go weeks without speaking to or seeing them. So it can feel quite isolating.

A perception also exists of what challenges are acceptable for leaders to talk about and what challenges you should keep in your thoughts or perhaps only share with a close loved one. In the first two chapters of this part, I get everything out in the open, looking at the spoken as well as the unspoken problems that can come with leadership.

I then move on to looking at how you might start to move beyond these problems, outlining the four stages of learning, along with the levels involved in the dynamic leadership journey.

CHAPTER 1
SPOKEN PROBLEMS

In this chapter, I share with you the problems leaders face and are comfortable talking about with their peers, their managers and even their teams. What's often missing when these problems are discussed, however, is the root cause or underlying driver. In other words, the spoken problem is generally the result of something else going on but that's often left unsaid.

Some of the spoken problems I hear from leaders are around:

- *Talent:* Leaders often complain that not enough talented people are applying for the roles. Or, they just don't meet company requirements.
- *Retention:* Leaders talk about how people just don't stay in jobs very long anymore. Or they may say something like, 'This industry is notorious for high attrition; we've just got to accept that as reality.'
- *Absenteeism:* 'Our unplanned leave is high because of the stress of the role,' leaders might say. Or, 'The staff are young and believe that taking this kind of leave is an entitlement.'

- *Productivity:* 'Staff are unproductive, lazy, time-wasters who aren't doing what they're supposed to.'
- *Industry:* 'Times are tough for our industry.'
- *Customer experience:* 'Customers are more demanding than ever; they just want more and more and more.'
- *Staff engagement:* 'Staff don't feel like they're receiving enough communication, so we need to throw more at them.' Or, 'We've got one "troublemaker" in our team who's pulling everyone else down.'
- *Resistance to change:* 'People don't like change.' Or, 'They're jaded from previous changes and the impact it had on the business.' Or, 'They're old-school and won't want to do anything differently.'

In the following section, I look at each of these problem areas in a little more detail.

Talent

I'm always curious about the term 'general lack of talent' and how it is determined. It's one of those throwaway statements that are often made without question, comment or challenge but that don't really tell us anything. Do leaders who complain about this as a problem actually know what talent looks like or how talent is defined? The dictionary meaning for talent is a 'natural aptitude or skill' but how do you define this specifically? What measures are you using and how do these translate to the role you're hiring for?

Given Australia's population and the frequency with which people change roles I struggle to see how leaders aren't finding talent. According to the Australia Bureau of Statistics, over 60,000 students finished secondary school in 2018 in Victoria alone. And according to University Rankings Australia, over a million students are pursuing university education across Australia. (For full details on these figures, see the Sources section at the end of this book.) Many of these students have entered the workforce in some capacity and I'm sure they have talent ... just perhaps not the experience you're after. So the idea that talented people are not applying for a role is certainly a sign to look a little deeper. Could the lack of applications be caused by the role itself or how it's being advertised? Could it be caused by the industry or the organisation specifically and the reputation it holds in the community?

As for applicants 'not meeting requirements', I do wonder whether leaders are looking to hire more versions of themselves or more versions of their highest performers. Or, are these requirements they're looking for experience-related? If so, they can probably be taught once the person is in the role.

When I finished high school and briefly moved to Bendigo to study (in a degree I can't remember the name of but was related to social work), I looked for part-time work to support myself. I had experience milking cows, picking fruit (including oranges, lemons, strawberries and kiwi fruit) and I'd worked in a roadhouse for three years while at school. I took my resume into 20 of the 52 pubs that were open in the area at the time, only to hear the same response: 'We only hire people with experience.' What?! How was I supposed to gain experience when no-one would give me a go? I was a quick learner and I know now that pulling a beer isn't rocket science, but they made it out to be a big deal. What bar tenders need are skills in working well under pressure, multi-tasking, smiling and using a till. I had all the skills they needed but because I didn't meet their requirement (to have specific bar experience) they overlooked me.

Now, you may argue that the skills required for your roles are more advanced or sophisticated than simple beer pulling, but this is rarely the case. Skills such as working under pressure and working creatively and collaboratively are transferable from many roles. Knowledge of job-specific tasks can be easily taught in the role.

Retention

Staff retention is another area rarely analysed in detail. How many leaders actually capture data around why staff leave? I know some organisations perform an exit interview when people leave but, while this is generally well intended, it's often poorly executed. It's usually conducted by someone from within the organisation, which creates an element of bias when seeking feedback. It's also performed on or close to the last day of the staff member's employment, when they've completely checked-out and are unlikely to care enough to give honest and open feedback. And, if by chance the leader does receive honest and open feedback, they rarely use it to make positive change and instead formulate a more palatable justification for their feedback and avoid taking any responsibility.

Here are some of the more common reasons for a person departing that leaders gravitate to (instead of seeking more meaningful feedback or analysis):

- They decided the role just wasn't for them.
- They weren't the right fit.
- They weren't capable of doing the work.
- They didn't have the right skills to succeed.

- They didn't get along with their peers.
- They weren't happy with the hours the job required.

Now I'm not saying any of these reasons are incorrect or are never a contributing factor in someone leaving a role, but it's worth exploring deeper reasons if you have high attrition in your team.

There's a saying that people don't leave organisations, they leave people. So if you were to entertain that thought, you may notice that you might have contributed to their departure. A lot of the time this starts with the hiring process. Consider how you advertise, interview, recruit and induct new staff. When you need to hire, do you reuse an old role advertisement that is outdated and no longer really relevant to the role itself? Or do you review it and make changes based on observations and feedback from your last hiring experience?

If you're not setting a realistic expectation of what new recruits can expect when they come to work for you, you're already setting your new hire and your team up for failure.

You're busy, I get that. You need staff really quickly, I get that too! But when you don't take the time to sell the role in the right way, you end up with people who don't fit. Perhaps you talk about how amazing your team is and how much the person will be able to contribute with their skills and experience. The successful candidate walks away thinking they've just scored the role of a lifetime and possibly found the place they'll live out the remainder of their working life. Then they're inducted. You bring them in and optimistically show them around the office. You introduce them to the team and everyone gives a little elevator speech about how awesome they are. You share the strengths of the new entrant and create excitement about having them on board. You continue the commentary around how great your organisation is but perhaps start to add in a little reality around your policies and procedures and codes of conduct.

Then, you sit the new entrant down and teach them how to be just like everyone else! They learn processes, policies, systems, team culture and business etiquette. And throughout this process, they receive one very clear message: 'No-one cares where you've come from or what you know. You're here to just do your job – like everyone else – so get on with it … quietly …please.'

So after the amazing build-up followed by a shattering crash to reality, you're left with a wounded employee – someone who's barely through their probation period and wondering if they've jumped out of the frying pan and into the fire. Someone who is already showing signs of disengagement – actually, at this stage, it's probably disappointment!

And, to seal their fate, you completely forget about their skillset and bring in consultants and experts to do the things you could have got your staff to do for free!

Then, they hand in their notice of resignation. They've been taught not to burn their bridges so they tell you something you want to hear and not the real reason they're leaving. And you let them go – none the wiser and ready to make the same mistake over and over.

What's also important to note around retention of staff is the cost associated with replacing someone. A lot of different research is available on this, but the general consensus is that replacing someone costs around 50 per cent of their annual salary.

Want to know how that's made up? Every time someone leaves your organisation, it costs you in:

- lost productivity – in the days and weeks leading up to their final day, many staff members simply take their foot off the gas and coast
- going away morning teas, lunches and so on – which can affect the productivity of a whole team
- recruitment and advertising costs
- time to create a role mandate and ideal candidate profile
- time to screen candidates
- time to conduct interviews
- time to give feedback and notify unsuccessful candidates
- time to conduct on-boarding activities (including aspects such as building passes and computer access)
- time to induct the new recruit
- training time and costs
- lost productivity while the new recruit becomes proficient in their role.

Absenteeism

Just like low retention, absenteeism costs businesses millions of dollars each year. And also like a high attrition rate, a lot of this cost is avoidable.

It's pretty obvious when someone is absent but it's not always clear why. Of course, we're all susceptible to the odd virus or common cold as the seasons change. But some employees will take leave on a regular basis throughout the year. So why is that?

I have worked with businesses that attribute high absenteeism to the industry or the nature of the work being performed (for example, the stress of contact centres and sales environments). And while I'm sure the industry and work has some impact on the health and wellbeing of staff, other businesses in these same industries or doing the same kind of work have quite low unplanned absences. So it's not okay to use the industry or type of work as a blanket reason when you have high unplanned absences in your team.

The other argument I hear (and have even used myself in the past) is that staff simply fake their illness. They don't come into work because they've had a big weekend or because they want leave but aren't confident a request for annual leave will be approved so they take sick leave instead. And I see businesses go to some pretty extreme measures to deter this behaviour. Some leaders will insist on having their staff call them directly (instead of texting or emailing) so they can interrogate them. Others will get staff to call a service such as Victoria's Nurse on Call to validate a medical condition, or require a medical certificate for even just one day of sick leave (this is often only required if staff call in sick on a Monday or Friday).

I've also seen leaders put staff through a gruelling 'return to work' interview once they're back from sick leave. Their leader will sit them down and ask if everything's okay and if they need any support. And while the intention of the interview can come from a positive place, the delivery makes the process uncomfortable and sometimes quite intimidating.

When staff are absent, a leader definitely feels an increase in pressure to maintain output and productivity. Over time, this can lead to resentment and frustration, not only for the leader but also for the remaining staff who need to work harder to cover the gap. So when conducting these types of 'return to work' interviews, or even asking a returning staff member how they are feeling, a leader's frustration can often be seen and felt by the staff member.

There are times when we're legitimately unwell and times when we come to work and don't get much done (Fridays are the preferred day for this to happen). But if your staff are displaying symptoms of excessive absenteeism, there's likely to be a deeper issue. And most of the time this deeper issue is with their leader ... you!

Productivity

I love productivity as a measure because it gives a really good snapshot of how a team is performing. But the measure alone doesn't determine overall success, and it certainly doesn't confirm whether someone is lazy or wasting time. The overall success of a team depends on many other factors, including quality or work produced, time management, engagement, culture and relationships. To talk about productivity as a problem, you first need to understand how it works and then how it fits into the bigger picture.

How productivity works as a measure

Productivity measures how effectively someone performs an activity or task. Perhaps tasks are allocated a certain number of minutes or hours to perform, and staff are expected to complete a set number of those tasks in their standard work day.

For example, if a task takes an average of 45 minutes to complete and a staff member works for 450 minutes (7.5 hours), they should be able to complete 10 of these tasks in their day. If they did, this would make them 100 per cent productive. If 12 tasks were completed in the day, the average time taken to perform each reduces to 37.5 minutes, lower than the set 45. Productivity for this staff member would then be 120 per cent for the day. Similarly, if only 8 tasks were completed in the day, the average time taken to perform each task increases to 56.25 minutes, higher than the set 45. Productivity for this staff member would then be 80 per cent for the day.

Productivity isn't generally assessed on a task-by-task basis but as an average throughout the day and across a week or month. So if a staff member spends half of their month only completing 8 tasks per day and the other half of their month completing 12 tasks per day, their average tasks will still be 10 and their productivity result will still be 100 per cent.

The key dependency for productivity is the timing given to the task – in this example, 45 minutes. If the average time set for the task reduced to 40 minutes, staff who previously achieved 100 per cent productivity would now be at 89 per cent.

So before you can attribute productivity to performance, you must understand how it is calculated in the first place and whether it's still relevant to the success of the business.

Some of the areas of productivity that you might question when you move into your role are:

- *Measurement:* What tasks are we measuring? Are we measuring the right tasks? What isn't currently being measured that should be?
- *Timing:* How do we know the task should take the time we've given it? Did we simply take a guess? Did we time our quickest person once and use it as the benchmark? Or did we time all of our experienced staff a number of times and use the average?
- *Complexity:* When was the time last calculated? Has the complexity of the task changed over time, with steps added or taken out? Has the knowledge and expertise of

the staff we're hiring changed over time and, if so, what does that mean for the time we allocate to tasks?

- *Environment:* Has the workspace become noisier and does this affect the level of concentration staff have? Are staff dependent on other teams and are they easily accessible? Are their work stations set up correctly and do they have enough space?
- *Interruptions:* Are staff being constantly interrupted by other people or by notifications on their electronic devices (for example, emails, calls, messenger conversations)? Are they required to attend meetings, training or impromptu discussions? Are they expected to answer questions and coach newer staff members? How is this taken into consideration?

How productivity fits into the bigger picture

Productivity measurements give you a snapshot of what your team are accomplishing daily, weekly and monthly. Over time, productivity can help to tell a useful story – but it will rarely tell the whole story on its own.

Used effectively, productivity can indicate what areas need some attention and so help you decide whether training or coaching is needed. However, productivity figures should be accompanied by figures on utilisation, which measures the amount of time a staff member spends doing the tasks required over the unproductive time (for example, time spent in meetings or in training).

High productivity can be just as problematic as low productivity. If your team have consistently high productivity and high utilisation, it could lead to burnout and an increase in absenteeism. If your team have high productivity but low utilisation, it might be a sign that you're over-investing in training at the expense of completing tasks.

So, using productivity measures effectively is all about understanding the metrics, learning to see patterns and seeing the whole picture – and not just looking at productivity in isolation.

What if I don't measure productivity?

Some leaders, particularly those in smaller businesses, don't measure productivity but simply base it on observation or gut feel. This is dangerous!

Let's look at some examples. Say Jane is on her phone whenever her leader sees her. You may assume she's not being productive. Similarly, if there's a lot of chatter taking place in the team, you may assume it's work-related and the team is being highly productive. However, if you're not measuring productivity, you really don't know.

It is so easy for all of us to 'look' busy, but if we're spending our time performing unnecessary tasks or performing necessary tasks over a longer amount of time than is needed, we're being unproductive.

It's often those who look the busiest who are the least productive overall – but without a measure, you just don't know. For you to understand whether your staff are productive, you first need to define what productive looks like in your business. To do this, you need an objective metric that staff can use as their own measure for performance.

Industry

Blaming 'the industry' for how your team is performing is a really easy way to avoid what's really going on. It's kind of like the ostrich sticking its head in the sand – it closes you off to all other possibilities.

Some issues that are blamed on the particular industries they emerge in, and the way these issues are dismissed, include:

- *Customer experience ratings in the banking industry:* 'Customers don't trust banks, they think the bank is only interested in money so we're never going to improve the experience.'
- *Low retail sales:* 'Times are tough for retail; no-one's spending any money in stores, people are now buying online; everyone's experiencing the same thing.'
- *Attrition rates in contact centres:* 'Staff don't stay long in contact centres so we don't even worry about trying to retain them.'
- *Employee engagement in hospitality:* 'The work is hard and the pay is low, so engagement isn't ever likely to be high.'
- *Reliability in construction:* 'No tradie is ever organised or on time; that's just the way it is.'

But if you go deeper on each of these, you will see that the issue being presented isn't actually the problem that needs to be addressed. For example, customer experience ratings in the banking industry might be improved through better communication, management of expectations and knowledge of staff.

Sales in retail stores might be improved if staff were more focused on the customer entering the store than what a colleague did with their weekend. Okay, that may have sounded dismissive, but let me pause here for a brief rant … I am not a big shopper. Even before I had kids, I wasn't a fan of shopping with no specific intention. If I need something, I go to the shopping centre with an idea of which stores might be able to help me and then go straight to them to see if they have what I need. Recently, I needed to get a new pair of boots; it was winter and my feet were getting cold with the shoes I had. I went in to a large and well-known department store and headed for the shoe department. I spent seven minutes looking at boots and trying pairs on – during which time, I wasn't approached by a single store attendant. I found a pair that fit well and the price was right. I was ready to buy. I looked around the store and saw a number of attendants, all looking very busy even though only a handful of customers were in the area. I waited for another four minutes, boots in one hand, wallet in the other, ready to buy – and was unable to capture anyone's attention. So you know what I did? I put the boots down and left the department store, without saying a single word to anyone. If a retail business can have a customer in their store for over 10 minutes without any contact, I don't think the issue is with the industry. I then went to another shoe store (a smaller one) and was immediately greeted upon entering. The store attendant asked if I needed any help to which I replied, 'Yes, I need a pair of boots.' She showed me to the boots section, helped with finding the right pair and with sizing – and ended up convincing me to purchase not one but two pairs of boots. All of this was done within seven minutes. No issue with the industry, just an issue with a particular store.

While I agree that certain challenges are more evident in certain industries, (often made worse by the media attention they receive), you can't leave it at that and let things stay the same. You may have to work harder to overcome these challenges, but that's what differentiates you from your competitors.

From a leadership perspective, the challenges experienced when managing people aren't specific to industry. We are all dealing with people and people have similar issues and needs regardless of the industry. So when it comes to improving performance and retaining staff, the capabilities of the leader are what make the difference.

Customer experience

How your staff treat your customers is a reflection of how you treat your staff! Yet when leaders talk about poor customer experience in their business, they often look for gaps in processes and systems. They think improving customer experience means giving customers more and continually doing better than competitors. And while there's an element of this, customers really just want to feel heard, appreciated and respected. Interestingly enough, that's also what your staff want.

I love Richard Branson's motto that 'If you look after your staff, they'll look after your customers.' I can definitely see the importance of this when I think back to my days working in a pub in the United Kingdom. Every morning when my boss pulled into the carpark, I would feel a wave of anxiety flow through me. *What mood is she in today?* I would wonder. The second she walked through the door, I knew if she was happy or angry – and I'm pretty sure those were the only two emotions she displayed.

On the days when she was happy, she had a spring in her step. When she said 'hiya', she would make eye contact and smile, she would engage in conversation, ask how we were feeling and have a laugh. The mood of everyone on these days was upbeat and full of fun and excitement. The day went quickly, customers were happy and so were we. It was on these days that we loved working in hospitality, and that feeling of togetherness and being part of something greater than ourselves. It didn't matter that we were going to be run off our feet for the next 12 hours, because we felt appreciated and valued. The challenges that came with our role seemed insignificant and we genuinely enjoyed ourselves – and the customers on these days tipped more and complained less!

Compare that with the days when my boss was angry – when she walked through the door with her head down, and when she would avoid eye contact and move quickly. If you were listening carefully, you might hear a mumbled 'hiya' as she stomped through to the office, where she would remain until the kitchen opened. Sometimes she would venture out to question one of the bills for the previous night and often this felt like an interrogation rather than an act of curiosity.

She never bothered to control how she was feeling, and this would have a direct impact on all her staff. One night after closing, she had a little too much to drink and got into an argument with her husband, who was really good at not giving a shit. She was trying to get her point across and he continued to dismiss what she was saying. Eventually he went home and she was left seething. She launched the gin glass she was holding across the room and it shattered into a thousand pieces on the floor. That was where it remained until the next morning. That day was particularly worse than normal. She came in puffy eyed and ignored us completely for most of the day.

Another time I remember her having an argument with the chef. She was so furious with the conversation that she started pulling plates off the shelf and smashing them on the floor. I remember that day clearly because it was a Sunday, our busiest day of the week. I also remember running out of plates and needing to dig some old ones out of the back storage room so we could continue to serve food.

Of course, the mood of everyone on these days was one of caution. There was no play, no laughter and certainly no fun or excitement. We were careful not to make mistakes or to be seen to be enjoying ourselves too much. If we did ignore her moods on these days and attempt to remain upbeat, she would give us crappy tasks or make us do things over. She was also really quick to look for our faults and let us know when we weren't doing things the 'right' way. She would make snide remarks and could make us feel like the most insignificant people in the world. On these days, we watched the clock, counting down the minutes until the end of our shift. Our approach to customers was formal and unwelcoming, and we had higher complaints, fewer tips and everything felt a lot harder than it needed to be.

What's interesting is that my boss never saw herself as the problem. She was completely unaware of her emotions, and how they affected her behaviour and the behaviour of those around her.

I remember wanting to leave that job so badly but having to wait an extra three months until my working holiday visa to Canada came through. I didn't want to be there, I felt stressed every morning when I woke up because I didn't know how the day ahead would go, and I stopped caring. When I eventually left I was desperately unhappy and couldn't wait to see the back of the pub.

What I've noticed when working with businesses to improve culture and customer experience is that if staff aren't feeling valued and appreciated, they will make it really hard for customers to interact with them – not intentionally but as a by-product of how they're feeling. The effort for customers to remain may become greater than the effort to take their business somewhere else, and a lot of the time this is what they'll do.

One of the biggest opportunities to improve customer experience, and so retain these customers, isn't to continue to give them more and more and more. It is to make it easy for them to deal with you and your staff – reduce their effort. And to do this, you must make it easy for your staff to deal with you, because they are a reflection of how they're treated.

Staff engagement

Many organisations run an annual employee engagement survey to determine how happy (or unhappy) their staff are. Over a number of weeks, staff are perhaps sent a link via email to respond to the survey. They are then required to answer a variety of questions about how they feel in relation to the organisation, their direct manager, their team and the broader business.

The responses are collated, de-identified and then presented to the business with recommendations and insights around the consolidated results. These types of engagement survey reports can provide some valuable sources of information on what the business is doing well and where blind spots might exist in relation to their staff.

Where the survey is not so helpful is when leaders fail to take responsibility for the role they've played in the engagement of their staff. Ideally, a leader wants their engagement to increase year on year, and some will go to enormous lengths to make sure that happens. I recall a leader in one team who bribed and threatened his staff to respond to the survey positively, even standing behind them as they completed it. He didn't remain with the organisation too long but also never saw value in the survey and what he could learn from it as a leader.

I'm actually not sure if I took these kinds of surveys too seriously when I was a new leader. They felt like just another 'tick-the-box' activity. We would know the approximate month the survey was going to be delivered and in the month prior we would run staff development training, hold team lunches and rewards nights, and even offer chocolate to those who completed the survey. It was a big focus to make everyone feel appreciated, once a year! After that we would go back to normal, with achieving results the priority and staff engagement the afterthought.

What bothered me most about the survey was when I was completing it myself, as a leader. One year I went through the survey and answered as honestly as I could. I included feedback about my leader and the areas where I thought he could improve, with the main area being communication – not a strength of his. Of what I experienced, he wouldn't share information with us and when he did it was well outdated. He was unclear on the long-term objectives of the business and, when I queried him about this, would tell me that this wasn't the kind of business that needed a vision or a direction. He would fail to let his team know when someone new started, and instead an introduction email would generally come out the week after they'd commenced, when everyone had already met the new person. I remember when I left the team, I even drafted my own farewell email so he could simply make tweaks and send it to the team. So I wasn't surprised when the findings of the engagement survey came through with communication being one of the key areas for improvement.

With the report being consolidated (to remain confidential), it not only had the results of feedback from my manager's direct reports but also feedback from my direct reports – and therefore the actions were delegated to us to correct. So I was appointed to lead a working group to improve communication across the business, which was an issue I had with my own leader!

As such, the issue that I had around my manager's communication was never actually addressed. The solution to the problems involved doing more – for example, creating a monthly newsletter and sending weekly updates and providing more detail. The actual problem, however, wasn't so much the quantity of communication but the quality and how it was being delivered. Again, the response was to tick a box and make it look like we were taking the feedback seriously but it wasn't a surprise when 'communication' was still an issue in the following year – only this time it wasn't me who gave the feedback. Knowing I'd be left running working groups to solve any engagement problem that emerged from the feedback, I lied on all surveys after that point – it wasn't worth the effort.

So while engagement surveys can be fabulous, a degree of governance and integrity sits with you as the leader to make sure you're doing the right thing and addressing the real problems. You also have an opportunity to take responsibility for how you may have contributed to the engagement of staff.

On the complaint of 'we've got one "troublemaker" in our team who's pulling everyone else down', I think all teams also have a crusader; someone who's willing to put themselves out there to make things right. If you have a troublemaker in your team, you have a wonderful opportunity to learn from them. They will be the one willing to tell you how they're feeling and what's frustrating them. Many leaders simply want the troublemaker out of their business, but if they do this they're missing a big opportunity to listen, understand and then make things right. Your biggest troublemakers can become your biggest crusaders and advocates if you take the time.

Again, this relates to the previous section. If you look after your staff, they will engage and do what's needed to ensure your success and the success of the business.

Resistance to change

As a natural default, most of us opt for taking the path of least resistance, and of doing things the way they've always been done. If we've been doing things a certain way for a long period of time, they become automatic and use less energy – we often don't even need to switch our brains on to perform them. They are habitual and unconscious.

So when staff don't want to change, it's usually simply a matter of not wanting to fix something that doesn't appear to be broken. If something's working fine now, they may ask, why are we wasting time and energy on doing it a different way? Thinking like this doesn't make staff resistant to change, it just makes them comfortable with how they're doing their job.

To fight this resistance and comfort, you need to encourage your staff by highlighting all the benefits that will come with a new way of doing things. For example, how will the changes reduce effort and give them time back? Or how will they keep their jobs secure in the future?

The challenge with change in many businesses is that leaders don't spend the time communicating with staff about what they're doing and, more importantly, why – they simply roll the changes out and expect staff to conform. Depending on the individual, some staff will be okay with this approach and others will absolutely not. Consider people's core needs around certainty and uncertainty, shown in figure 1.1.

Figure 1.1: Certainty versus uncertainty needs

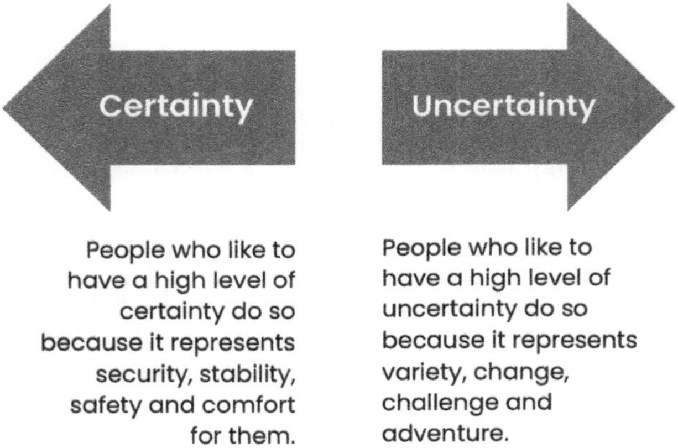

Certainty
Uncertainty
People who like to have a high level of certainty do so because it represents security, stability, safety and comfort for them.
People who like to have a high level of uncertainty do so because it represents variety, change, challenge and adventure.

Staff who like certainty and are thrust into change without notice or enough information will appear to be resistant or averse to change. Leaders who aren't aware of these core needs and don't prepare their staff accordingly will feel the pain as they try to fight the resistance. And even if the change is implemented, there's a high likelihood it won't be adopted longer term.

The thing that makes the difference to your staff accepting and embracing change is whether they trust you or not. Do they know you well enough to know that you have their best interests at the centre of the decisions you're making? Do they truly believe you care enough to protect them from change that's not relevant or suitable? Are they comfortable that you will keep them safe and secure in their role?

If you don't have the trust and respect of your team, any change is going to be a challenge to implement. You will be met with resistance at every step of the way. It will feel like you're rowing upstream. Staff may say they agree but that doesn't equal full support on making the change successful. They won't commit; instead, they'll sit on the fence and, if given the choice, they'll let it fail. This will be their lesson to you to do it properly next time.

When your team trusts you and believes that you care about them, only then will they care about you and the business. Seriously, this isn't rocket science but I'm always surprised by leaders who don't think they're part of the problem when it comes to the implementation of change.

The other thing to point out when it comes to successfully making a change in your business is this: if you're not 100 per cent on board with the change, you're likely to sabotage it without consciously being aware of it, and you will be the reason the change fails. As a leader, if you can't rationalise the change, you're unlikely to convince your staff to get on board.

Once you've made sense of the change (which could require some clarification from third parties) your attention can shift to convincing your staff. This is the part that takes the most time – and is often the part leaders will try to speed up or skip over.

According to research conducted by Prosci (experts in change management – see www.prosci.com) one of the main reasons staff resist change is a lack of awareness, followed closely by fear of the unknown.

So remembering that it's not that people don't like change but that they don't like to be changed means you are in control of the outcome. The key is choice. No-one likes to be forced into doing anything, including me. The second someone says to me, 'You don't have a choice, you have to do it', I feel all my muscles tighten, my breath becomes shallow and my face starts to go a little red. I feel cornered and that generally triggers my instinctive response of 'fight' (others may take flight or freeze in this instance) and I'll argue using as many angles as possible, even if they're unrealistic and make no sense at all – and I am even not above an adult tantrum if the circumstances are right.

This concept of being given a choice rings very deeply with me. I remember when I was about 10 years old and Mum was taking us to do the grocery shopping. We lived about 45 minutes from town and only did the shopping once a fortnight, so it was kind of a big deal, where we got out of our gumboots and made an effort to look good. On this trip, Mum insisted I wear a pair of maroon corduroy jeans that I absolutely detested and she said looked 'beautiful' on me. I huffed and puffed and pleaded to wear something different and eventually she pulled the Mum card and said, 'I'm not asking. Put them on and get in the car!' My fight mode was triggered, so I stomped into my room, put the stupid jeans on and crawled under my bed, because there was no way I was making this easy for her.

I heard the movement around the house as everyone continued to get ready and then Mum started calling us all into the car. I just stayed under the bed. I was hopeful that she would forget about me and I could stay under the bed all day. The last of the footsteps left the house and I heard the key turn in the lock. Then I heard Mum ask my siblings, 'Where's Shelley?' A few seconds later I heard fast and heavy footsteps walk onto the verandah, the key turned in the lock again and the door was thrown open. Mum stormed into my room and found me under the bed (my room was really small so there weren't many hiding places). She started with the demands, telling me to get in the car 'or else', but I held my ground. She realised her approach wasn't working and so softened, begging me to come out. I resisted as much as possible until she changed approach again and threatened to tell my dad. That was the one thing I wasn't risking, and was enough for me to get out from under the bed and hop into the car. I wore those ugly maroon corduroy jeans that day with contempt. There was no way I was making them look good and I wasn't about to make Mum look good either. I moped around the shops, shoulders slumped, with a permanent frown on my face. When I got home that afternoon those corduroy jeans were put in a hidden place, never ever to be seen again … Mum had won the battle but I had won the war!

Now I have my own children I feel the pain and frustration my mum felt and I appreciate her intentions so much more. But I also recognise the need for my kids to make their own choices. And I recognise the need to be patient and give them the opportunity to ask questions, and to understand 'why' they should be making the change. If they don't go ahead with the change, that's on me and my ability to influence!

If you have staff (or kids) who are avoiding change, think about how you engage them in the process. How much trust do you have with them and how much are you willing to challenge if you don't believe the change is right for your people?

Finally, resist the temptation to blame your staff and their 'resistance to change'. It's not that people don't like change; it's that people don't like to be changed. The key factor here is about choice. Increasing awareness will open up choice.

CHAPTER 2
UNSPOKEN PROBLEMS

I think all leaders at some point or another will question whether they are worthy of their position. Some leaders will do this on a regular basis and others may only do it when they are in their early stages of leading a team. For those who are overly critical of themselves, they may question whether they should be in a leadership position on a daily basis. It won't necessarily be something they externalise but can be something they think about and worry over continually. The doubt may rise up after they leave a meeting where they've been asked a question they don't know the answer to. Or it may creep in when they say good morning to a staff member who ignores them, when they don't get invited to an important meeting, or when they have to engage HR to formally performance manage someone in their team. These doubts and questions can prevent them from having the decent night's sleep they so desperately need to function effectively.

Others may not give their worthiness a second thought and assume that their role as a leader is something they are entitled to. They may think that they know how to be a better leader than anyone else and have nothing to lose in giving it a red-hot go. Their self-talk is purely around how well they're doing and that the problems they are facing are typical of leadership. They will justify their situation as being caused by 'the nature of the environment' that they are working in.

And at both ends of the spectrum come challenges. At one end, leaders overthink their worthiness and wonder whether the opportunity will disappear at some point. They really don't see all of the good things they bring to a role, and instead focus on what's not working well and how insignificant they are. And, at the other end, leaders may not see opportunity for improvement or how they're part of the problem. They may make decisions and take action that compromises their integrity for the opportunity to stand out.

In this chapter, we explore some of the problems leaders face but don't often share with others – in other words, the unspoken problems, the things that are keeping them awake at night.

Some of these unspoken problems are backed up with negative self-talk, such as:

- 'I'm not worthy enough.'
- 'I don't know what I'm doing.'
- 'I'm scared that I will make a mistake.'
- 'I'm afraid I will be embarrassed.'
- 'I worry about failing and I play it too safe.'
- 'I want to do what's right for everyone and I am struggling to maintain a balance.'
- 'I'm trying to be everything to everyone and I don't know how.'
- 'I'm not qualified.'
- 'I'm not good enough.'

... And so on and so on. These thoughts don't come from nowhere, and usually have deeper causes. So what we will explore a little bit further in this chapter are the unspoken concerns felt by many leaders around:

- *Not having the right training to lead:* Perhaps you feel like you've just been thrown into your leadership role and are expected to figure it out yourself.
- *Reacting to situations and struggling to get ahead:* Or perhaps you feel like you're constantly putting out fires and fixing things that are broken.
- *Not having the right conversations with staff:* Addressing challenges as they arise and not letting issues manifest may be another problem you wrestle with.
- *Doing the work themselves instead of empowering their people:* Perhaps you struggle with letting go of the need to deliver as an individual contributor.

Too often these kinds of spoken problems are presented with a really quick remediation activity that allows leaders to continue to take a 'tick-the-box' approach (similar to some of the issues discussed in the previous chapter). If we start to look at the unspoken problems in more detail, though, we can see some of the real challenges leaders face.

Not having the right training to lead

What makes individual contributors so successful in their role is, to a large extent, dependent on the training and support they receive in the early stages of entering a role. When they have a clear understanding of their objectives and the expectations required to be met to perform their role, and when they have adequate training and coaching, their success can come quite quickly. Similarly, to make an influencer or leader successful, they also need training and coaching; however, this area is often not given the same focus.

Looking at the usual transition into 'entry level' positions makes the move to leadership all the more shocking. It's not shocking as in appalling, but shocking as in having a bucket of ice-cold water thrown over your head!

When an individual contributor enters an organisation, they are inducted, trained (often both in a classroom as well as online) and eased into their work (with the support of an experienced buddy) over a number of weeks or months.

So it's not unrealistic that new leaders would expect the same type of transition into their role, particularly when they are first-time leaders. But what does this transition usually look like for a new leader? Is the focus on the task and how to have performance conversations with people? Or is it how to run a report and what to contribute in leadership meetings?

The idea of a leadership role, before you move into it, is often a lot different to the reality. You go from knowing everything and everyone and having confidence that you're a valued asset to knowing nothing and no-one and wondering when you'll be exposed as a fraud.

Outside of leadership, in very few roles would you be expected to learn as you go and just figure things out on your own. Doing so in most other roles would put the business at risk – from a customer experience, brand, reputation and compliance perspective. Without adequate induction and training for staff, customers wouldn't receive consistency of service and important compliance metrics may not be adhered to.

I remember my first day as a leader – sitting at my desk and wondering what on earth I was supposed to do with my time. I recall saying to myself, 'How on earth will I prove that I am a capable leader if I'm not actually doing any work?' And aside from a few hours of sitting with my leader and going through the reports I was responsible for generating, I wasn't actually given a great deal of guidance on how to become an influencer. And that's the transition leaders must make – the transition from control to influence. As an individual contributor, you are in control of your results, you are in control of your actions, and you are in control of how you spend your time. So moving into a leadership role and transitioning from control to influence is a big change and not one that you will learn straightaway.

Of course, for leaders to be formally trained upon entering a role isn't always realistic because they're often the only leader commencing their role at the time. One-on-one training is laborious and time-consuming so leaders tend to get a crash course and then it's merely a learn-as-you-go approach. Many managers will teach their leaders to do what they do. I know from my own experience that following my first leader at the time wasn't helpful at all. Indeed, following my leader led to a lot of the behavioural challenges that I faced later on. You see, my manager at the time was a very quiet, passive and introverted woman who had this gentleness that allowed you to relax whenever you were with her. Her own development was focused around assertiveness, confidence and pace – things I didn't have any issue with.

As I followed her style of leadership, I found myself wanting to do it even better so I could prove that I was worthy of being a leader. How this style came across for my team, however, was as overly assertive and overly confident, which led some of my staff to feel intimidated and belittled – which was definitely not my intention.

Without following the leader, however, how is a new leader supposed to learn to be influential and, ultimately, successful?

Leaders who have concerns around a lack of training should feel empowered to take the necessary steps to get what they need. This book is your first step to become a dynamic leader. The second step will be looking at ongoing opportunities to invest in training and professional development, either with the support of your business or on your own. When I was in my early 20s, I discovered the power of coaching from my older sister, Narelle. She would spend $150 each month to speak to a professional coach over the phone. At the time, I thought Narelle was a little loopy – why on earth would you spend $150 on a phone call? But I watched her grow and evolve in her career and I saw that by investing in herself in those earlier stages of her career, she grew quicker and went further than she would ever have without making that investment.

If you're a leader and you need training, you are 100 per cent responsible for ensuring that you get it! It is foundational and an investment that you will continue to reap the benefits from for years to come. Then you have an ongoing focus on building capability.

Reacting to situations and struggling to get ahead

A leader can go from sitting at their desk on day one, twiddling their thumbs and not knowing what to do with their time, to, by week two, feeling they can't find enough hours in the day to fix all the problems that need to be sorted out in the business.

How is it that leaders get to this point? I have no doubt that this is a question that many ask themselves at the end of a really long working day. Perhaps you also ask yourself questions like, 'What am I doing wrong?' and 'How is it that other leaders look so calm and composed and get everything done with such ease?'

When you're an individual contributor, you succeed based on what you achieve, or your output. So your natural gravitation when you transition into leadership is likely to be similar. Only because you're being paid more, you place a greater emphasis on output, and feel like you need to do more of the 'doing' in an attempt to reassure your managers that they made the right choice in promoting you and you are a good investment.

The problem is that working 'in' the business leaves you no time to work 'on' the business. So you end up only having time to react to situations rather than being proactive and overcoming problems before they arise.

The answer to becoming more proactive is based in prioritisation and time management.

I love the urgent/important matrix that was developed by Dwight Eisenhower, 34th President of the United States (from 1953 to 1961) and a five-star general in the United States Army during World War II. If anyone needed to prioritise what they did with their time, it was this guy! He used his urgent/important matrix to make sure he was focusing on the things that were important and not wasting time on the things that weren't.

His matrix (see figure 2.1) is really simple and super effective for sorting out where your focus is.

Figure 2.1: Urgent/important matrix

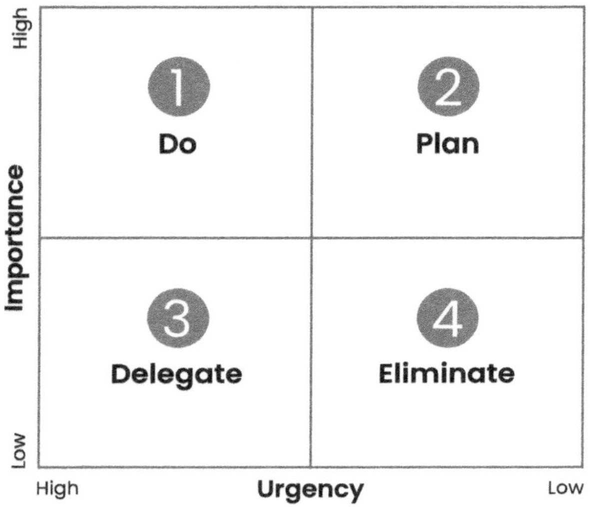

A reactive leader, who feels like they're constantly behind, is likely to be spending the majority of their time in quadrant #1 – that is, on tasks of high importance and high urgency that they just need to get done. These tasks are things like responding to a customer complaint, gathering data for a senior leader, fixing a core system that has stopped working or finding staff to cover unplanned absences in the team. Leaders in this quadrant will be frantically putting out these fires and responding to requests for the best part of their day, every day. With the little time they have left over at the end of the day or between urgent tasks, they will sit in quadrants #3 and #4 – that is, they will spend time doing things of low importance, that could probably do with being delegated or deleted – but they will feel like they're keeping busy.

Quadrant #3 are tasks of high urgency but low importance – things like changing the toner cartridge in a printer, ordering food for a team lunch, sending a weekly report to stakeholders or posting the daily mail. There's a time requirement but the importance is low and the task is likely to be quite easy (and mind-numbing) for a leader whose head is probably aching from all the tasks they've completed in quadrant #1. You should delegate these quadrant #3 tasks to someone in your team or, where possible, automate them.

Quadrant #4 tasks are of low urgency and low importance. I call this the 'cat videos on YouTube' box. Completing these tasks is a waste of time and energy and delivers no real benefit to the individual or business – it really is like watching cat videos on YouTube! These tasks include activities like sorting emails into sub-folders, rearranging your desk, colour-coding calendar invites with no real intention (albeit this activity could actually be for effectively managing time) or complaining to a colleague about the quality of coffee. If you eliminate these tasks, you then have time to spend working on the tasks that matter and will contribute to your longer term success – and, more importantly, your long-term sanity.

Quadrant #2 is where the magic happens. These tasks are important but don't necessarily need to be done right now. Focusing on them means you're working 'on' the business. They include tasks such as designing a clear strategy for achieving your objectives, outlining steps to execute on the business's strategy, communicating upcoming change and seeking input from staff, speaking with a staff member about certain behaviour that might be having an impact on the brand or having one-on-one conversations with your staff to talk about performance and how they're doing in life in general. A leader who sees the benefit in long- and short-term planning will begin their day in this quadrant – and will use their calendar to make sure the important but not urgent tasks are carried out. They will block out the first hour or two in their calendar, perhaps before other people arrive at work, while they have a good amount of mental energy, and definitely before all the other distractions creep in. They will see this quadrant as one that requires regular focus and daily attention, and will have the discipline to stick to it.

I love quadrant #2 – it's where a lot of this book was written. I had been chipping away at it for almost two years, doing a little bit here and there. What was great was the discipline I found once I'd locked in a publisher and had a timeframe for the manuscript. Right now, as I type these words, it is 4.10 am on Christmas morning. Santa has delivered the presents and they're waiting under the tree for my kids to wake up and open them in about three hours. I will work on my manuscript until the day begins and then I won't think about it again until 4 am tomorrow. You may think I'm crazy getting up at this hour, particularly on Christmas morning, but I am making it a priority because I know how much this book is needed. I know it will make a big difference to the programs I run and the longer term success of my business, and so I'm making time. Don't get me wrong – I'm not saying you should wake up at 4 am, but I am saying to make time for the important things, however that looks for you.

For new leaders, it's easy to come into the office in the morning and get lost in emails and reports and people coming to your desk and before you know it the day is over and it's time to go home. It's in these moments that you say to yourself, 'Where did the day go? I've still got so much more work to do.' I cover this in more detail in chapters to come. For now, know that reacting to situations and struggling to get ahead is a very real issue for leaders, and while some overcome it, many will not get past the challenge.

Not having the right conversations with staff

Since becoming a coach and a leadership trainer, I have been surprised at the number of leaders who don't know how to have an effective conversation. On reflection, this was also very evident when I was in the corporate environment, but I didn't make the connection until I started to focus on communication.

What's more concerning than leaders not knowing how to have an effective conversation is that they don't know they don't know. Many think they're great at communication – you're probably one of them! These leaders see no issue with how they communicate with their team and they're unlikely to have ever received feedback to the contrary. It's only when I scratch the surface and ask their staff how they feel about their ability to have an effective conversation that I – and these leaders – realise just how big the gap is.

Real-life example

I had recently had a coaching conversation with a leader who was thinking about firing one of their staff members. Here's roughly how it went:

Me: *So you're saying they're not doing what they're supposed to be doing?*

Them: *Yes, that's right; they're useless!*

Me: *Okay, so how do they know what they're supposed to be doing? Have you told them?*

Them: *Yes, they know.*

Me: *How specifically do they know?*

Them: *Because that's just their job.*

Me: *Okay, have you ever told them exactly what you expect of them?*

Them: *Yeah, it's what they were hired to do.*

Me: *Okay, but have you ever sat them down and taken them through what's expected in detail?*

Them: *Yes, of course ... well not really ... Isn't it just common sense?*

Me: *Perhaps it's common sense to you but I'm tipping they might not see things in the same way. Have you ever given them feedback?*

Them: *Why should I need to give them feedback? This is what they've been hired to do!*

Me: *Okay, so if I hired you to be my admin person, would you know exactly what was expected of you?*

Them: *Um, no, but that's different. Admin is really broad. This job is simple.*

Me: *Would your job be simple to me, if I had never done it before?*

Them: *Okay, so you're saying I shouldn't fire them?*

Me: *No, that's not what I'm saying, but I am wondering how much of the problem lies with you. If they don't know what you expect because you've never told them and you're not giving feedback, they're not really set up for success are they?*

Them: *Okay, so I need to talk to them?*

Me: *Yes, it would definitely help to talk to them and be clear on what you expect. And perhaps ask some questions to understand what they expect.*

For the remainder of the coaching session, we worked on having the actual conversation. And what the leader originally thought was common sense was actually really difficult to articulate and put into words.

We talked about the words 'we' and 'you' and 'I' and how using these words in the wrong context can have a significant impact on performance. When a leader uses 'we' in a one-on-one conversation, the other party is likely to assume that there's no action or change that they need to make. 'What can we do to improve your performance?' implies that someone else is responsible for making the change. If you change the question to 'What do you need to do to improve your performance?' the person you're asking this of knows 100 per cent of the responsibility lies with them. A simple tweak to just one word can be the difference between an effective conversation and an ineffective one.

The other challenge around having effective conversations is the fear that we might upset someone or they'll see it as a form of conflict. Most people don't like conflict and will go to some interesting lengths to avoid it as much as possible. Unfortunately, this leads to the avoidance of some simple conversations that would be helpful for the development and success of their staff.

Real-life example

Jane has just joined Kate's team and was hired because of her bubbly personality and positive energy. Throughout the first month of Jane being in the team, Kate noticed that Jane regularly interrupted her peers when they were speaking. Kate assumed it was her passion for the job and willingness to show what she was capable of. Kate said to herself, 'This is just a phase; she'll be fine once she settles in.' She doesn't say anything to Jane.

Jane continues to interrupt and speak over her peers over the next three months and staff have started to withdraw and avoid conversations with her. Kate has also received a number of complaints from customers calling Jane bossy and rude. Kate decides she needs to speak with Jane about her communication and arranges a time to meet with her.

The conversation is very relaxed and casual; Kate tells Jane that she's a valued member of the team and she really likes her levels of enthusiasm. She says in a joking, light-hearted tone, 'We have received some feedback from our customers about how we're talking to them. We get so excited sometimes and we can forget to give the other person a chance to speak. I know I do that occasionally, but it's really important that we hear what they have to say, don't you think?' Jane agrees with her comment and the conversation comes to an end with both parties leaving feeling positive. Kate believes she's delivered feedback on Jane speaking over people and Jane believes Kate is happy with her levels of excitement. Nothing changes.

Over time, Kate starts to resent Jane for her behaviour and the impact it's having on the team. Jane is completely unaware of what Kate or the team think about her behaviour and just carries on as normal.

Eventually, Kate engages HR and decides to put Jane on an informal performance improvement plan. She receives help on what to say and how to say it and arranges the meeting with Jane. The HR contact offers to come along to support the conversation. As Kate delivers the information in a formal, pre-written script with an HR representative sitting beside her, Jane appears completely shocked. She had no idea of the impact she was having on her peers and also her customers. She left the meeting knowing what she had done wrong but wondering why this was the first time she'd been given the feedback. Why didn't anyone say anything earlier? Her sadness soon turned into frustration that Kate had brought in an HR person to their conversation and that the way she had delivered the message was really cold and uncaring … what had happened?

Jane's behaviour around talking over people improved dramatically after the conversation with Kate and HR, but she disengaged. She no longer spoke in meetings and her energy was flat. She took sick leave on a regular basis and withdrew from the team. Kate assumed that Jane was upset about the feedback and again assumed it was a phase that would pass. But it didn't ...

After a number of vague, indirect conversations with Jane about her targets and the work she was doing, Kate again engaged HR and initiated another informal performance improvement plan. Jane was less shocked during this conversation but her disappointment was clear. She accepted the feedback and a few weeks later handed in her resignation.

Kate never questioned the role she had played in Jane's performance and subsequent departure from the organisation. She believed she'd done all the right things as a leader and never addressed the effectiveness of her conversations. Of course, this kind of reaction and rationalisation meant it was only a matter of time before she would have to go through this with another person in her team!

Like Kate, new leaders are at risk of letting a molehill turn into a mountain before they address the issue. Conversations that are avoided, however, bubble away under the surface and do real damage to trust and the strength and resilience of a relationship over time. So, having the conversations regularly and authentically will mean a good outcome for everyone!

If you're worried that the conversations you're having with your staff aren't effective, you're probably right! And it will not only be affecting your staff but also having an impact on your brand across the business.

> *While no single conversation is guaranteed to change the trajectory of a business, a career, a marriage, or a life, any single conversation can.*
>
> **Susan Scott**, author of *Fierce Conversations*

Doing the work themselves instead of empowering their people

How many times have you felt overwhelmed since becoming a leader? How often have you said to yourself, 'I wish the work would just stop for a minute so I can catch my breath'? How easy are you making it for your staff to continually look to you for all of the answers?

It's such an easy and tempting choice for leaders to just do the work themselves, and many get sucked into a vortex that is very hard to remove themselves from.

You know you should be delegating and empowering your people but, as you look through your 'to-do list' for opportunities, you find all the reasons why 'this' task should be done by you. You may say to yourself:

- 'This is easy; it will only take a minute.'
- 'It's too hard to train someone; I will just do it myself.'
- 'I don't have time to teach them; it will be quicker if I do it.'
- 'I'd probably need to re-do this myself anyway, so I may as well just do it to begin with.'
- 'No-one can do it like I can.'
- 'I can't risk them getting it wrong.'

I'm sure you can think of others. You will rationalise all these reasons and be happy with the decision you make, but you'll still be overwhelmed and the work will still keep coming! The reason you're happy with your decision is because it brings short-term, temporary relief. Ticking a task off your never-ending list of things to do feels good. What's important to realise, though, is that delegating work is a long game – while it's not one with short-term benefits, it has many more benefits over the long term. If you're going to delegate – which I strongly recommend if you're going to succeed as a leader – you have a choice to make.

I'm not going to tell you there's a quick way to delegate tasks, or one that doesn't require you putting in time and effort – that would be a lie. What I will say, though, is if you are delegating a task, you need to understand that the pay-off will be in the long term and not the short term.

To delegate effectively, you will need to spend time with your staff, teaching them what you know, and helping them to understand why the task needs to be done in the first place. You will also need to let them know what factors are important in the completion of the task and not simply assume they'll know. For example, your task may require an unusually higher level of detail than others might expect, so you would explain what is required and why in the beginning. If the task needs to be done by a certain date in order to achieve an overarching outcome, this also needs to be communicated. If new systems need to be learnt or new terminology needs to be used, time will be required to teach the staff member and allow them to ask questions and seek clarification.

The delegation of tasks will rarely deliver benefits the first time they're performed, so make sure the person you're delegating to will be available in the future. The second time the task is performed, you should see a small benefit and by the third and fourth times, you should be able to stand back and allow the staff member to do the work themselves with minimal or no support. The great part about delegating is that when the staff member becomes proficient, you can get them to teach the next person and so you really only need to go through the process once.

Before you dismiss delegation as an option, I want you to consider how much more effective you will be in your role if you're not spending time on things that aren't that important.

Depending on your leadership level, industry and role type, delegating work could see a 20 to 50 per cent improvement in your performance (see Thomas Hubbard's article 'Delegating more can increase your earnings – full details in the Sources section at the end of this book), which means greater success to your business and the organisation overall. Leaders who delegate are given the next opportunity, because they're operating at a higher level!

It is important to understand that continuing to do the work yourself will continue to increase your workload. Over time, this can lead to burn out and disengagement. It is here that I see a lot of leaders experiencing a lack of confidence in their abilities, and they start to question their worthiness. They are so busy doing the work that they don't really see any way forward.

To add to the pressure, leaders are expected to continue to improve year on year. In order to do this, you have to find ways to work smarter and not simply work harder.

So part of new leader development is around delegation and having confidence in your abilities and the abilities of your staff.

In the next chapter, I outline the stages a leader goes through and the decisions you need to make to help determine whether you succeed or fail.

CHAPTER 3
THE FOUR STAGES OF LEARNING

In this chapter, I think it's worth sharing with you the four stages of learning, which was first described in 1969 by management trainer Martin M. Broadwell. It is used in psychology and by trainers to describe the stages we go through to learn a new skill. I have adapted the model for use when coaching leaders to help them to understand the journey they are on, both mentally and emotionally.

Becoming a dynamic leader involves skills that are learnt over time. This is a journey that takes longer and requires more energy from some than it does from others. No matter how quickly or easily you progress on your journey, however, you will transition through the same four stages of learning – from being unconsciously incompetent to being unconsciously competent. If you look at these four stages of learning, shown in figure 3.1, you will see that the amount of effort required as you progress through each of the stages varies.

Figure 3.1: The four stages of learning

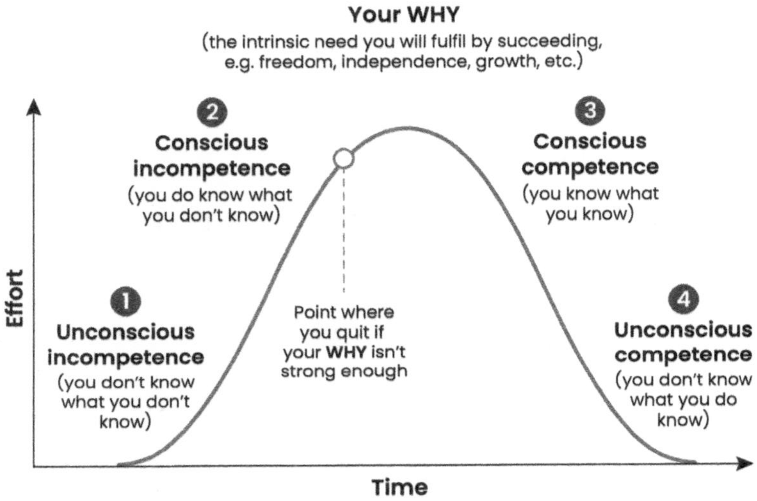

The following sections outline the four stages in more detail.

Unconscious incompetence

Before you became a leader and were looking in from the outside, no doubt leadership looked pretty easy. Think back to when you first entered the workforce. You may have looked up to leaders with envy, and desired to one day be like them and become a leader yourself. From the outside, a leader often looks confident, in control and in a position of power – at least, that's what I remember with my first boss. As you worked with your leaders over time and got to know them, perhaps they also came to look a little too relaxed or be a little too bossy. Some leaders can make their job look really easy and can come across as being a little lazy. You may have thought to yourself, *Wow! Being a leader means you can tell other people what to do and not do any work yourself, and you get paid more for doing it. Sounds perfect!* Many of us aspire to reach a position where we don't have to work too hard.

This is the first stage of learning, called 'unconscious incompetence' – or the stage where you don't know what you don't know. This stage is similar to sitting in the passenger seat as a child, watching mum or dad drive the car and noticing that they don't seem to be paying a great deal of attention to actually driving the car. They are able to have a full conversation with you at the same time as commenting on the environment around them and listening to the radio. And you still manage to get to your destination safely and with minimal effort.

Conscious incompetence

It's not until you get into the driver's seat that you realise just how much effort is involved with actually driving a car and getting to your destination safely. This stage is known as 'conscious incompetence', or where you now know just how much you don't know. For leaders this is generally days 1 to 60 in the new leadership role, where each day is different and you're learning just how much you didn't know about leading a team. Part of this not knowing is the technical side of the role, but mostly it's the interpersonal side – keeping your team motivated and dealing with the constant range of issues and emotions that arise.

Continuing with the driving analogy, you enter conscious incompetence as soon as you start the car for the first time. If learning on a manual, you are told to put your foot on the clutch and gently ease it out as you simultaneously use the other foot to press slowly down on the accelerator. Your instructor (likely your parent) will tell you not to ride the clutch (you have no idea what this means) and put just enough pressure on the accelerator so as not to stall (you also have no idea what this means). Suddenly there are all these components to driving that you weren't aware of and the effort is so high; and after riding the clutch or stalling the car one too many times you question whether you really need to get your licence.

It didn't look hard from the outside and now it is and is this even what I really want? It's at this point that you need to have a really clear understanding of WHY you actually want to get your driver's licence. When I ask my clients why they got their driver's licence in the first place, the most common response is 'to gain independence' with the next being 'for convenience'. For those who never get their licence, they either have different intrinsic needs or these needs are already fulfilled in another way. So they might give driving a go but quit when the effort gets too high.

The unique thing about leadership is that you don't have someone sitting beside you for the first 120 hours (the required number of supervised driving hours a person under 21 needs before they can sit their driving test in Victoria). You're lucky to have someone with you for eight hours. So the effort is higher and the reason you're doing it is so much more important. What will being a leader intrinsically give you? Your WHY needs to be intrinsic for you to remain on the journey – if you are just becoming a leader to earn more money, the increase in effort will likely be higher than what the money represents, and you'll quit. If you intrinsically want to be the best version of yourself and see the journey as representing success, you will have a strong enough reason to keep going.

If not, you're unlikely to make it past conscious incompetence, and instead you'll quit. You'll say to your friends, 'I'm not built for leadership' or 'It's not worth the sacrifice' or 'I'm happier just doing this' … and you'll go back to a safe and comfortable role and shut the door on leadership.

Conscious competence

Only over time and with practice and repetition can you move into the next stage, known as 'conscious competence', or where you now know what you know. This is achieved by repeatedly doing the same tasks over and over and over until you're no longer having to be reminded of what to do or supported in how to do it by others. You are very aware of what you're doing but the process is still quite manual and methodical. For a leader, this stage is supported by the development of a routine or a rhythm. You understand what you need to do daily, weekly, monthly, quarterly, half-yearly and yearly, and you know who needs what and by when.

You perform these tasks with intention and you're very deliberate in your actions. You still feel a little clunky in the early stages until you have performed the task enough times for you to relax and start to do it with ease (while still needing to consciously perform it).

When driving, conscious competence looks like this:

1. Walk around the car, check the tyres.
2. Get in the driver's seat.
3. Adjust the seat.
4. Adjust the mirrors.
5. Put your seatbelt on.
6. Make sure your passengers have their seatbelts on.
7. Put your foot on the clutch and brake.

8. Start the car.
9. Put the car into gear.
10. Indicate your direction.
11. Check your mirrors.
12. Release your foot off the clutch and simultaneously accelerate.
13. Drive.
14. Check your mirrors.
15. Change gear.
16. Check your speedometer.
17. Check your car's temperature.
18. Change gear.
19. Check your mirrors.

You get the idea. It is the breakdown of each component of driving a car that allows us to successfully pass our test and get our driver's licence. Our actions are deliberate and we know at what point we need to perform each action. We are able to follow instructions easily and do what is required to successfully pass.

For leaders, however, there is no test; your success in the role is not a pass or fail. There's rarely even a great deal of feedback to indicate whether you're on the right track. To succeed through this stage, you will benefit from having a strong support network, made up of colleagues who have been in leadership longer than you, a mentor who can provide guidance, and even a coach who can help with the transition and give feedback on possible areas for development.

Unconscious competence

Over time, and with a whole lot of repetition and feedback, you move into the fourth stage of learning, known as 'unconscious competence' – that is, where you don't know what you know. For a leader, this is where things start to feel easy, the effort reduces and things start to become automatic. You know what you need to do in order to succeed and you don't need to think too deeply or for too long before you take action.

In the driving analogy, think about your drive into work or drive to the supermarket this week. Do you have a conscious recollection of how you did it? How many times did you check your mirrors? How many red lights did you stop at? How many red lights did you go through? That last question might be scary to think about, but rather than consciously going through the motions, it all happens automatically or unconsciously. (So I'm sure you stopped at every red light!) This leaves space in your conscious mind to think about other things. While you're driving, you might also plan out the day ahead, go over a conversation you've had or are about to have, take phone calls, sing to songs on your playlist or listen to audiobooks. You do all this at the same time as driving and with much less effort than it took in the beginning.

Different roles have different levels of complexity, and progressing through the four stages of learning will vary from role to role. Learning to make an apple pie, for example, might only require a small amount of effort and the progression to unconscious competence might happen over a short period of time. Compare this with learning to be a paramedic, which would require a large amount of effort and might take years to master.

For leaders, the transition is going to be more like becoming a paramedic than it is learning to make an apple pie. So get comfortable with being uncomfortable! Or as Muhammad Ali says, 'Don't quit. Suffer now and live the rest of your life as a champion.'

CHAPTER 4
THE DYNAMIC LEADERSHIP JOURNEY

In this chapter, I share with you the different levels a leader experiences in their journey to becoming dynamic. By 'dynamic', I mean a leader who has a positive attitude, is full of energy and new ideas, and manages constant change, activity or progress really well.

Without a clear understanding of people who have moved into this kind of dynamic leadership, you are much less likely to succeed. The key here is to understand the journey and consciously choose whether you're going to make it a success or whether you're going to give up and let the leader within you fail.

Figure 4.1 shows the different styles a leader might progress through as they move up the leadership ladder.

Of course, not all leaders will make it all the way to 'dynamic'. In the following sections, I take you through the default approach for each leadership style, the amount of potential they're reaching and the areas that a leader needs to focus on to progress to the next level.

Figure 4.1: Styles of leader and the leadership ladder

Approach	Style	Potential	Focus
Invested	Dynamic	90 to 100%	Progression
Empowered	Influential	75 to 90%	Strategy
Structured	Collaborative	60 to 75%	Intention
Exhausted	Responsive	40 to 60%	Rhythm
Withdrawn	Dysfunctional	20 to 40%	Direction

The responsive leader

Approach	Style	Potential	Focus
Exhausted	Responsive	40 to 60%	Rhythm

In chapter 2, I outlined some of the unspoken problems leaders have, and I shared with you one of the challenges leaders have around being reactive and struggling to get ahead. If you're struggling with this challenge, you're sitting on the 'responsive' stage on the leadership ladder. Your leadership style is reactive and your approach is likely one of exhaustion – perhaps not in the beginning but definitely within the first six to nine months.

I'm starting with this leadership style because this is where a leader starts their journey.

Often when an individual contributor is performing at their peak and seen to have talent or potential, they are promoted into a leadership role. They have been really successful at achieving results within the team and are often subject matter experts (SMEs). They are promoted into leadership positions without analysing their ability or attitude to lead, and without them knowing how to influence those around them.

I remember my own transition into a leadership role (which I talk a little about in the introduction to this book) and how this compared to my transition into my first individual contributor role with the organisation.

As an individual contributor, my transition into the role looked like this:

- *Day 1:* I was inducted, given an overview of the business and its direction and how my role fitted in with this. I learnt about business values, codes of conduct and how to function in my team.
- *Day 2–21:* I spent three weeks in training, learning about aspects such as processes, systems, legislations and customer demographics.
- *Day 22–30:* I was put into a simulated environment where I practised my tasks with the support of a trainer or SME.
- *Day 31–35:* I was let out on the floor, where I sat at my own desk and a buddy would watch everything I did and be there for support.
- *Day 36–90:* I flew solo, but still sat next to my buddy so they were close by if I had any questions.

- *Day 91:* I became proficient and no longer needed the support of a buddy, and I was moved to another desk so the next new entrant could take my place.

Having exposure to a number of organisations, this is a very common process that works well for many businesses and for their new staff members. This is also how I trained staff myself. Never, ever, did I hire someone and put them straight to work – that would have been disastrous for our customers, our business and our team culture.

Yet ... this is exactly what most organisations do when bringing in a new leader. A leader's transition generally looks something like this:

- *Day 1:* Sit with manager to learn systems and reporting.
- *Day 2:* Sit in on one-on-one meetings with manager to see how it's done.
- *Day 3–90:* Attend way too many meetings and run between tasks scrambling to get things done. Address concerns and speak with HR (multiple times). Meet with manager as needed and figure it out as you go.

While I don't have any particular issue with promoting high-performers, I think businesses need to reassess how they're transitioned and the capability they're building in them over time.

I see how responsive leaders struggle to work *on* the business, spending way too much time working *in* the business. Without the right support, you cannot be expected to accomplish what you were initially promoted to achieve.

For me, the responsive stage of leadership was one of the loneliest times in my career. Because I'd been promoted within my existing team, I went from doing the work one day to allocating and making sure others (my former team mates) were doing the work the next. One day I was an individual contributor, achieving high results, having fun with my peers, not taking things too seriously but showing definite enthusiasm and promise. I was in charge of my results and, as long as I got the work done, I would succeed. The next day I was responsible for the performance of an entire team. The same people I used to have fun with were now looking to me for direction and guidance. Instead of just focusing on getting my own work done, I needed to inspire and motivate the people in my team to deliver.

The transition is definitely more mental than it is physical. When the only way you know to succeed is to continue to do the work, it's almost impossible for responsive leaders to resist the temptation. And along with continuing to do the work, you're also now responsible for running reports, attending meetings, addressing staff issues and handling escalations and complaints as they arise.

Your days of leaving work at work become a distant memory as you scramble to take control of the ever-increasing workload. And because you were successful as an individual contributor, you put pressure on yourself to be everything to everyone. You don't want anyone to think you were the wrong choice and, because of your drive for success, you'll do anything to avoid failing!

You're afraid to ask questions or say you don't know for fear that doing so will limit your career. Besides, your manager looks way too busy so you dare not bother them.

Rather than seeking support, you do what you can to get things done. You work harder and longer than ever before and you feel like you're treading water in rough seas without a life jacket.

As shown in the leadership ladder, a responsive leader is only operating at 40 to 60 per cent of their true potential – but the only way they know how to improve is to work harder. Doing this over time leads to exhaustion and potential burnout.

Responsive leaders almost run into meeting rooms and as they sit down they let out a sigh, like they've just completed a five-kilometre sprint. They are often distracted and respond too quickly to questions about their team. They can be defensive and quick to judge. They can also be very guarded and, therefore, not be embracing their true self.

I have coached a variety of different leaders who have been 'responding' for so long that they don't actually see any other alternative to success. A lot of the time, they don't realise how much they have contributed to the problems they're dealing with. Without being consciously aware of it, leaders often encourage staff to approach them at their desk 'anytime' they need help with something. They end up being the leaders who are approached 'all of the time' with questions from staff that, if they just switched their brain on, could solve the problem themselves.

If you're a responsive leader who's ready to move up the ladder, one of the best questions to ask yourself before doing any task is, 'Will this set my team up for success and help them grow and develop in the future?' If the answer is no, you're not investing attention where it's needed. If volumes are high and resourcing low and you're feeling the pressure of doing the work too, great – have a chat with a peer to see if they have any people they could lend you to help alleviate the pressure. Don't fall into the trap of rolling your sleeves up and doing the work because that will become your default every time and over a longer period this doesn't set you or your team up for success.

From the responsive stage a leader can go one of two ways. They can either seek the help they need to work smarter – to develop rhythm and structure and move up the ladder – and learn to float. Or, they can withdraw, stop trying so hard and sit back and coast, and move down the ladder – and sink.

Before looking at what happens if they move up the ladder to the structured, collaborative leader, let's first look at what happens when they move down the ladder.

Be strong enough to stand alone, smart enough to know when you need help, and brave enough to ask for it.

Unknown

The dysfunctional leader

Approach	Style	Potential	Focus
Withdrawn	Dysfunctional	20 to 40%	Direction

A dysfunctional leader is withdrawn, and this withdrawal happens mostly because they've burnt out – physically or mentally, or (most likely) a combination of both.

When a leader burns out physically, they have been working really long hours over a prolonged period of time. They have been the first person to arrive at work in the morning and the last person to leave in the evening. They have been eating meals from a vending machine and their gym membership hasn't been used in months. They drink each night and have started to put on weight. Their immune system is low because of the constant stress and they pick up every bug that comes into the workplace. They are tired all of the time and spend most of their weekends either sleeping or catching up on emails.

When a leader burns out mentally, it is the result of ongoing stress and them not feeling like there's a way out. They will have made sacrifices in some personal aspect of their life and have a constant feeling of guilt mixed with the overwhelm of all the things that need to be done. Perhaps their long hours have meant missing quality time with family, for example, or have put a strain on their relationship.

When burnout occurs, a leader may say to themselves, 'I've been working my arse off, I'm making sacrifices and I'm not even getting recognised for the hours I'm putting in. All I get is more work, not even a thanks.'

This is usually the tipping point that makes these leaders say, 'Enough is enough' before giving up completely. Their reason for becoming a leader in the first place is long forgotten and their number one concern is their health – they've entered survival mode. They will decide to only work the standard number of hours and no more. They will reconcile themselves with the fact that some things will no longer get done and often their overall standard of performance will decrease – but this is the trade-off they have to make.

From the outside, a dysfunctional leader looks like a 'seat warmer' – someone who shows up but doesn't achieve much more than keeping the seat warm. They might run required reports, attend compulsory meetings and work on rostering but aside from that they'll do little else. They don't seem to be particularly interested in what's going on and won't run team meetings unless they absolutely have to. One-on-one conversations, if they happen at all, will be a tick-the-box exercise where the leader will do 90 per cent of the talking and the staff member will pretend to listen. The leader is unlikely to be addressing any performance issues with their team and the culture in the team will be apathetic, disengaged and unmotivated. Staff will treat customers with little more interest than their leader treats them and this will have an impact on the business. These teams are often underperforming or just meeting the standard.

Dysfunctional leaders are operating at only 20 to 40 per cent of their full potential and this will have been noticed by their peers and stakeholders. They are looked upon by their team as ineffective and some may wonder how they got the role of leader in the first place. I know I've certainly asked myself that question about certain leaders a number of times in the past. That they could get away with doing nothing, day in day out, used to annoy me. Now I'm saddened by it.

What I know of the leaders I've worked with is that rarely are dysfunctional staff promoted into leadership roles. The transition to dysfunctional occurs once they're in the role and haven't had the support or knowledge needed to succeed.

You see, most high-performers who become leaders expect that they'll have all the guidance they received when they entered the organisation in the capacity of an individual contributor. They expect that their leader will guide, mentor and train them to become successful in their role. When this doesn't eventuate, they slowly withdraw and become dysfunctional, and by this time they've convinced themselves that they're not cut out for leadership. They don't want to work the long hours and believe the only way to stop doing so is to either find another role or withdraw. They often won't talk to anyone about their challenges for fear they will look stupid or be involuntarily removed from the role. They will question how they became so successful in their individual contributor role and beat themselves up about failing in this role.

Internally, they'll conclude they're a failure but won't externalise it; they'll just keep it bottled up. Some may blame their own leader for their failure and put the responsibility outside of themselves – 'They gave me too much work', 'They don't understand the challenges of my team', 'They're never around', 'They don't give me any support' and so on and so on. They'll say to themselves, 'This isn't worth it' and, again, if they don't have the right guidance or support, they'll continue to spiral downwards.

To instead move forward and upwards, dysfunctional leaders must first decide whether they want a future in leadership. Then they must work out their direction. What do they want in their career and is that with their existing organisation or another one? Then they need to be prepared to seek the support they need and take control of their career.

The collaborative leader

Approach	Style	Potential	Focus
Structured	Collaborative	60 to 75%	Intention

To transition from the responsive style to a collaborative style (or jump up from the dysfunctional style), a leader needs to find their rhythm. And to do this, they will need support. This may be in the form of online learning, a book (like this one), a conversation with their manager or a peer, or through attending leadership training (like the Dynamic Leaders Tutelage).

Rather than reacting to all situations, as you progress to a collaborative leadership style, you can start to anticipate regular events and plan a structured response. These events may differ slightly from business to business but could include:

- part-time university students needing time off for exams
- increased annual leave at popular times like Easter and Christmas
- higher volumes aligned to seasonality trends (which will be different for each business)
- increased sick leave during the colder months
- scheduled system upgrades.

As you start to anticipate and plan for these kinds of events, you may decide to adjust rosters and put certain projects on hold so as not to increase the impact of a particular event. You may employ and train a pool of casual staff in readiness for high leave periods. Or you may speak with a peer in another team and see if they have excess resources you can borrow, with the intention of lending back during quieter times.

One of the organisations I worked for implemented a workforce management system that allowed leaders to balance their focus around cost, quality and time. These three areas are known as the 'triangle of objectives' (originally created in the 1980s by Dr Martin Barnes) and are interrelated in that focus on only one area will affect the other two (see figure 4.2). The key is to balance your focus in all three areas.

In this organisation, leaders spent time coming together each week to look at resourcing, incoming volumes and targeted completion rates. They looked at teams that were working way too hard on a Monday and not achieving much at all on a Friday, and talked about ways to balance the workload so it was consistent throughout the week. They looked at how time affected (or didn't affect) quality and adjusted delivery metrics to ensure a good balance between both. And they explored ways to get maximum value out of employees without blowing the budget.

Figure 4.2: The triangle of objectives

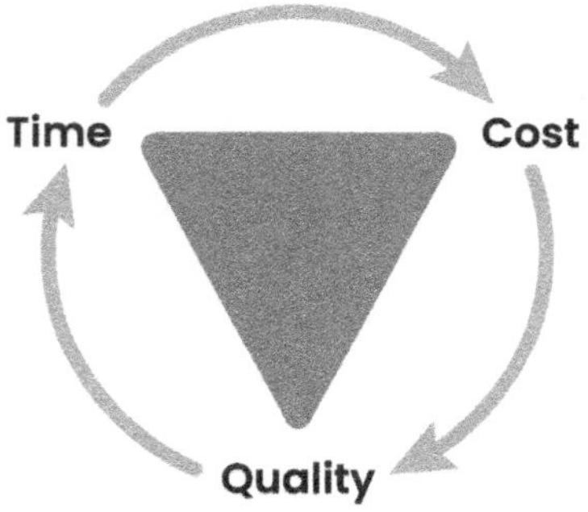

Prior to using a workforce management system, leaders would offer overtime to staff whenever there was a backlog. They would pay them to work longer hours and even come in on the weekends. Offering overtime rates comes at a great cost to an organisation, particularly when you consider the reduction in productivity when staff are working longer than normal hours. They found a better solution was to borrow staff from teams with like-for-like functions, and get their help in clearing the backlogs. Having the skills required meant that staff would need to be trained in advance, so leaders needed to be proactive and organise this training before the backlogs arose. The other solution was to increase their staffing levels with casual staff so that when the work was there they were brought in and when it was quiet they weren't used. A lot of the teams adjusted their mix of permanent and casual staff as well as their full-time and part-time ratios.

Using this type of structure in the business provided really clear visibility about the current and future state of the business, and allowed leaders to work on the business and work more cohesively with their peers. They were forced to collaborate, particularly when the option of overtime was removed!

Collaborative leaders learn to bring other people in and seek their support in fulfilling responsibilities and overcoming challenges. They aren't fearful of losing their position or looking stupid if they ask for help or make a bad decision; instead, they are open to being vulnerable and accept that leadership is an ongoing learning journey. Leaders who adopt this mindset are much more likely to remain successful in the future.

Of course, successful collaboration takes time, and requires openness and the space to have conversations about possibility. Collaboration is not about having a discussion with someone else about a solution you've already committed to. To effectively collaborate, a leader must be curious about other perspectives outside of their own world of understanding. And to do this, they must also have the patience to listen and ask questions. I expand on these ideas throughout the book.

So knowing collaboration takes time, patience, openness, curiosity and an element of vulnerability, you can no doubt see how a leader who is responsive and reacting to their workload may struggle to do it effectively, if at all. Instead, they may try to convince themselves that they already do it well, but their definition of collaboration doesn't really hit the mark. They may see collaboration as merely asking someone else for their opinion, even if they're not particularly interested in their response. They may pretend to listen, nod and feign interest, but then take no notice of what is said and continue with their original plans.

The structured, collaborative leader stage, however, is the first stage where you can start to work smarter and less hard, and move to working at between 60 and 75 per cent of your full potential. You're opening up to the idea that you can succeed through others and that not everything has to be done by you or to your standard. You can start to build foundations and take a longer term view on the benefits small changes will bring to the business over time.

To transition to this next level of influence, you must focus on intention. That is, you must know why you're doing *everything* that you're doing. If you're having a quick chat with someone in the kitchen, for example, it's because you understand the importance of building relationships and the more people you know, the greater likelihood you'll receive support if you ever need it in the future. If you let a staff member leave early for an appointment and still pay them for this time, you know that staff member will be more likely to stay back to help during busy periods.

The collaborative leader already sounds pretty good, but let's take a look at the influential leader!

The influential leader

Approach	Style	Potential	Focus
Empowered	Influential	75 to 90%	Strategy

Once a structured leader is intentional about their actions and collaborating well with peers, staff and stakeholders, they will then transition into the influential leader phase.

Influential leaders have let go of the 'command and control' style of leadership and, instead, inspire their people to be the best versions of themselves. They spend more time asking than they do telling and believe that their views, opinions and ideas are just some of the many possible perspectives that exist. They move from being really involved in making the decisions to stepping back and empowering their people to make the decisions independently. They teach their staff to assess the risks and benefits when making decisions, and support them when things don't go as planned.

It's impossible to move to a position of influence if you're still controlling all decisions and are knee-deep in doing the work yourself. To transition into a truly influential role, you need to let go of some of your immediate responsibility and trust that your team can succeed independently and with little input.

When this shift takes place, your awareness of yourself can't help but expand and your thinking evolve. You become more aware of the things you 'do' rather than the person you 'are'. For example, I previously saw myself as a passionate person but now see myself as being passionate about certain things. Being a 'passionate person' implies that I'm this way all of the time, which I'm not (particularly when it's time to do the laundry!). Being passionate about certain things, however, demonstrates my awareness of what I'm capable of and can access in certain contexts to help achieve results.

Dr Robert Kegan, a developmental psychologist and author from America, calls this the 'subject/object shift'. In his book *Immunity to Change* (see Sources at the end of this book for full details), he says that, 'Any way of knowing can be described with respect to that which it can look at (object) and that which it looks through (the 'filter' or 'lens' to which it is subject)'. This split between subject and object can be further explained as follows:

- *Subject ('I AM'):* Self concepts we are attached to and thus cannot reflect on or take an objective look at. They include personality traits, assumptions about the way the world works, behaviours and emotions.
- *Object ('I HAVE'):* Self concepts that we can detach ourselves from, and which we can look at, reflect upon, engage, control and connect to something else.

Kegan talks about the subject/object shift in reference to the theory of adult development where we transition and transform through five stages of development with each stage building off the last. We move what we 'know' from subject (where it is controlling us) to object (where we can control it).

It is through empowering your staff and becoming influential that you can create the space to step back and consider how effectively you are running your team and your business. At this stage, you can really start to realise your potential and operate at between 75 and 90 per cent. You can utilise your resources effectively and create the opportunity to work on your business as opposed to working in it.

When as a leader you are working *on* your business more than *in* your business, you can shift your focus to the bigger picture, the strategy. What is it that you want to achieve in the future? What do you want your team to achieve in the next year? What will the team look like and what kind of work will they be doing? And what actions need to be taken in order for it to happen?

As adults, when we transition into the influential phase of leadership, we also transition between two of the stages of adult development: the socialised mind and the self-authoring mind. These can be defined as follows:

- *The socialised mind:* This is where what you think to 'send' out to people will be strongly influenced by what you believe others *want* to hear. Leaders at this stage will be influenced by groupthink and may even omit sharing information if they think it may not be well received.
- *The self-authoring mind:* This is where what you send is more likely to be a function of what you deem others *need* to hear to best further the agenda or mission of your design. Consciously or unconsciously, you have a direction, an agenda, a stance, a strategy and/or an analysis of what is needed, and a prior context from which your communication arises.

Some leaders can actually also achieve a third stage, which is the self-transforming mind, but this is unlikely in the early stages of their career. According to Dr Kegan, the self-transforming mind 'can stand back from its own filter and look *at* it, not just *through* it'. A leader at this stage will both value and be wary about any one way of looking at things. Kegan says that 'people with self-transforming minds are not only advancing their agenda and design. They are also making space for the modification or expansion of their agenda or design'.

In addition to progressing through to a new stage of adult development, an influential leader will begin thinking proactively about who will step into their role when they move on. They will start to put a succession plan in place and intentionally develop the capabilities of key staff within their team.

Now let's look at those at the top of the leadership ladder – the dynamic leaders.

The dynamic leader

Approach	Style	Potential	Focus
Invested	Dynamic	90 to 100%	Progression

Dynamic leaders are fully invested in the success of their people and the success of their business. They are in complete alignment, and all of their decisions and actions support this. They understand that their individual success is dependent on the success of the people around them.

Dynamic leaders are completely comfortable with giving the credit to the people around them and assuming more than their share of the responsibility when things don't go as planned. They see failure as an opportunity to learn and grow, and they've let go of most of the fear associated with it.

Leaders who take credit for the work of others or blame their staff when mistakes are made don't make it to this level. These leaders are a different type of dysfunctional and their time in leadership is limited. They may be promoted from role to role but this isn't reflective of their leadership style, and is likely based more on the illusion they've created around their abilities. Generally these leaders 'manage up' really well, and they learn to tell people what they want to hear, even when it's not necessarily true. They let their ego drive their decisions and do so at the expense of others. I've often wondered how these leaders get to this stage and I can only conclude that they've followed the wrong leader!

At the dynamic stage, a leader's workload lightens, because they aren't putting so much pressure on themselves to deliver individually. They are utilising their resources and focusing on leadership, strategy and building the capabilities of their people. Once you reach this stage as a leader, you're operating at or close to your full potential. You are ready for the next opportunity and are starting to set yourself up for the move.

Your focus should also shift to growing your networks and building your brand, both within and outside of your organisation. It is at this stage that you may also decide whether your future as a leader is more 'I' shaped or 'T' shaped. Are you going to be a specialist leader who understands a lot about a little – and so the 'I' shaped leader? Or are you going to be a generalist leader who understands a little about a lot – 'T' shaped?

If you're going to specialise and become an 'I' shaped leader, your focus will be more on the subject matter and building expertise around the specifics of the area you're interested in. For leaders in the project space, this might involve honing in on a specific type of project – for example, technology. It would mean gaining exposure to projects that fit your interest and going deeper in your understanding of concepts and environment. You might invest in training in the methodologies for technology projects, like SDLC (software development life cycle), PMBOK (Project Management Body of Knowledge) or Prince2 (PRojects IN Controlled Environments), to name a few. You may then look for opportunities to put the newly learnt methodology into practice to gain experience. 'I' shaped leaders will remain in a particular field or industry, and build out their expertise through knowledge more than capability.

In contrast, if you're going to generalise and become a 'T' shaped leader, your focus will be less on the subject matter and more on your capabilities. You will need to go wide. While 'T' shaped leaders have the ability to go deep when they need to, for the most part they will operate at a higher level. They will rely on their staff to know the detail and pay attention to what's happening across the broader business. They will be interested in a wide range of themes – from operations and finance, to product and marketing, to sales and even to risk and compliance. They will be curious about the different nuances and areas of focus each business has and look to gain experience across a number of businesses.

As a 'T' shaped leader, your opportunities are unlimited – provided you plan well in the early stages of your career. Rather than focusing on vertical transitions (for example, team leader to manager to head-of), you would look for horizontal transitions (for example, team leader of sales to team leader of operations, to team leader of risk) and gaining as much exposure to as broad a range of roles as possible. This makes it easier to go deep when you need to with greater ease.

With this focus, you would invest in learning more about the things that can be transferred between roles, business, industries and organisations. You might do a Master of Business Administration (MBA), for example, or train in change management, learn about emotional intelligence or how to create high performance teams. You might get a mentor who can teach you about how their business operates.

'T' shaped leaders need to have a greater level of awareness and be able to adapt to different environments in different ways. They are leaders who are always curious and have a never-ending desire to learn and grow.

Both leaders are important to business and the broader economy, so it doesn't really matter which way you go, as long as you know what that is. It's at the dynamic stage that you can make this decision and work on a longer term plan for your own career. What might the next opportunity be and how does it align with your choice of leadership styles?

In the chapters in the following parts, I explain in much greater detail how dynamic leadership works, breaking down the Dynamic Leadership model and focusing on each individual aspect.

PART II
THE OVERARCHING AND UNDERPINNING LEADERSHIP THEMES

Businesses with dynamic leaders perform better than under any other type of leader. They have fewer performance management issues, higher engagement, better customer experience and overall cost less to run.

Dynamic leaders also understand that they're not finished in their learning journey and must continue to evolve and adapt to remain relevant in the future.

For leaders to progress to the dynamic stage, two themes must be front of mind at all times. The first is what I refer to as the 'overarching theme' of communication – while communication is generally something we do automatically and take for granted, it is something that you must become more conscious and deliberate about if you're going to succeed in the other areas I cover in part III of this book.

The second theme is what I refer to as the 'underpinning' theme of time – our most precious commodity and the one thing we can never get back. Time is possibly the most undervalued resource. We have enough of it but we waste a lot.

Figure 5.1 picks these two themes out from the Dynamic Leadership model.

In the following two chapters, I share with you how communication and time are foundational to leaders becoming dynamic and building high-performing, sustainable and engaged teams.

Figure 5.1: The overarching and underpinning themes

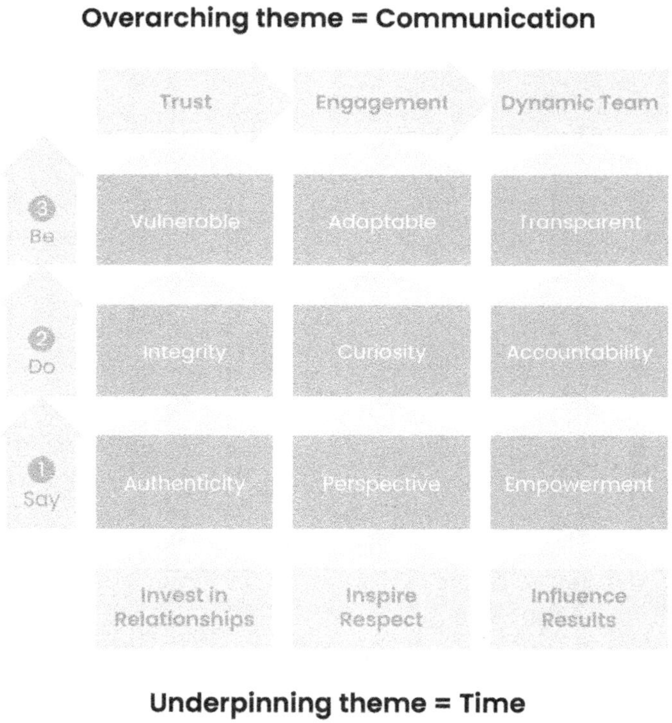

CHAPTER 5
OVERARCHING THEME: COMMUNICATION

As a kid, I remember being told to 'treat others the way you want to be treated'. I would often hear 'Shelley, you wouldn't like it if someone did that to you so don't do it to them, okay?' Sure, that's great advice in the context of the playground, but as an adult I've become really annoyed with it!

You see, if you treat me the way you want to be treated, there's a good chance you'll annoy me in some way. Not at first, perhaps, but definitely over time. Why? Because I'm not you – I don't think like you, my values aren't the same as yours (similar, perhaps, but not exactly the same) and how I communicate is likely to be different. So by treating me the way you want to be treated assumes we are the same – and we're not! We're all very different. We are who we are today because of so many variables: the house we grew up in, our siblings, how our parents raised us, the impact of our teachers, the influence of our friends, our experiences and what we made them mean, and so, so many other things.

How each of us views the world is different, which is why the approach of treating others the way *you* want to be treated may not be working that well for you right now.

So how do you treat others the way *they* want to be treated? Well, even though we're all vastly different, you're likely to be able to observe some common themes in others. To do this well, however, requires an increase in your awareness. Start paying attention to things you may have ignored up to this point. And when you notice things that are important to other people, adjust your style to copy them slightly. Not in a creepy or obvious way, and not in a way that takes you away from being authentically you. Just tweak your approach.

To help you in understanding how others might wish to be treated and communicated with let me take you through the three ways we communicate: verbally, tonally, non-verbally, bearing mind the following:

- *Verbally* – that is, the words we speak – comprises 7 per cent of our total communication (according to research conducted by Albert Mehrabian and outlined in *Silent messages: Implicit communication of emotions and attitudes* – see Sources at the end of this book for full details).
- *Tonally* – 38 per cent of our communication is tonal.
- *Non-verbally* – a whopping 55 per cent of what we communicate to others is non-verbal.

I also look at written communication, focusing mainly on email.

Verbal communication

If the words we use form just 7 per cent of our overall communication, we could be paying attention to a whole lot more. But let's not discount the importance the words hold or ignore some of the challenges they present.

When speaking with someone, either face to face, over the phone or via video conference we usually don't consciously give much thought to words. We simply open our mouths and let them pour out. We know what we want to say and will use whatever words comes to us in the moment.

It's only when the conversation is with a person of importance or around a sensitive issue that you likely become aware of the words that you're using. You might then think about your words more carefully and consider which ones to use. For example, when speaking with senior leaders, you might try to use complicated or more sophisticated words to show that you're intelligent and worthy of the role – words like 'extrapolate' and 'scrutinise'. Or when the topic is sensitive, you might use vague words to soften the message and avoid offending the other person – words like 'should', 'could', 'would', 'perhaps' and 'maybe'.

Both approaches can have the desired intention but can also discredit you if used incorrectly. In the following section, I list some other obstacles words present, and outline how these can be addressed with a little awareness.

Level of information provided: Big picture versus detail

Most of us have a preference for the amount of information we want to hear or share. Some of us like the 'big picture' analysis and others like the detail. So if we're given the wrong level of information according to our preference, we're likely to get frustrated with the conversation or switch off.

When communicating in big picture, you provide headlines or high-level snapshots of the message you want to deliver. Most senior leaders prefer this level of information and won't want to know the detail, so they don't provide it unless asked.

When communicating in the detail, you provide a lot of information. You might do this, for example, when communicating with someone in technology to solve a problem. You provide a step-by-step account of your issue, what happened and when, because it is only from the detail that the tech support person can identify the problem and provide a solution.

If you're not sure whether someone prefers big picture or detail, always start with the big picture and go from there. As you get to know people, you will be prepared with either more or less information. Just notice how smoothly the conversation runs when you adapt the level of information to suit the listener. Oh, and if you're feeling uncomfortable about the level of information you're giving because it's not your preference, don't worry – that's perfectly normal. Just keep going!

Considering those with English as second language

Speaking with someone who has English as their second language, and particularly if their English isn't great, requires a lot of patience and thoughtfulness. When I lived abroad I spent a lot of time visiting countries where English was not the residents' primary spoken language.

I had to really pay attention to what I was saying and keep my language as simple as possible. Conversations took longer and, at times, I really struggled to find another word for the one they didn't understand. The process could become time- and energy-consuming and a lot of times I gave up, deciding I really didn't need to know the answer to my question.

Even here in Australia, we have many residents who have English as their second language so being aware of the words you're using will have a positive impact on the quality of your conversation.

Keeping in mind age and skill level

Just recently I was having a conversation with my three-year-old daughter, Eva. We had taken her to a splash park earlier in the day and to begin with she hated the water and wouldn't go near it. My husband spent 20 minutes persuading her to get in, and then she finally went in and loved it. Afterwards, I commented to her, 'How awesome that you persevered at the splash park, Eva!' She responded with, 'What did you say, Mum?' I repeated my statement and again she asked me the same thing. Without thinking I repeated my comment a third time – to which she responded, 'Did you ask me a question?'

It was then that I realised she didn't understand what the word 'persevere' meant. And with her vocabulary still developing, she also didn't know how to respond. What her responses meant were, 'Mum I don't understand what you're saying.'

So I reworded my comment to, 'You didn't like the sprinklers to start with but you liked them in the end, didn't you?' to which she responded, 'Yes, Mum, I loved the sprinklers. Can we go again?'

This is just one of many examples where the language I've used has been too complex for the person I'm speaking with, and it's not just children who can struggle to understand. If people aren't continually expanding their vocabulary or subject matter expertise in the area you're discussing, they may only ever use quite simple language or not understand the terms you're using (see the following section for more on this), and there's nothing wrong with this. It is your responsibility to adapt your language to suit your audience and have the patience to persevere.

If you have young children, I have no doubt that you're reminded of this on a regular basis.

Avoiding corporate jargon

A number of articles have highlighted the use of corporate jargon and just how ridiculous we sound. After decades of being exposed to corporate jargon, I'm guilty of still using it myself at times. But the problem with jargon is that it can work to exclude those who don't know what it means.

Here are just some of the words that may be confusing to your listeners:

- 360-degree thinking
- bandwidth
- best practice
- break down the silos
- build consensus
- circle back
- core competencies
- customer centric
- deep-dive
- due diligence
- early adopters
- insourcing/cross-sourcing/outsourcing
- key takeaway
- learnings
- low-hanging fruit
- mission critical
- negative growth
- one-off
- one-pager

- paradigm shift
- push-back
- risk averse
- strategic fit
- sweet spot
- synergies
- table the discussion
- take it offline
- take the lead
- touch base
- value-add
- you've got your lines crossed.

Ask yourself what you really mean when you use jargon, and then say that instead!

Australian sayings

While English is Australia's primary language, we have morphed it into something that is uniquely ours. It's very Australian to abbreviate words or names that are long and lengthen words that are short, or do both. For example, my birth name is Shelley, which is often abbreviated to 'Shell' and then lengthened to 'Shelby', 'Shell-Dogg', 'Shell-meister' and 'Shell-grit' (thanks Grandpa for that one). Most of the time we do this when we like someone and it's a term of endearment but we must be careful not to offend by becoming too familiar if we don't know the person that well.

Along with lengthening and shortening words and names, we also use phrases that, when taken literally, can mean something completely different to what Australians know them to mean. Let me share an example of when this has happened.

My South African husband migrated to Australia in 2005 after we'd spent time living in London and Canada, so while English wasn't his first language he had learnt to speak it really well. What he wasn't prepared for when he came to Australia were some of the sayings we use on a daily basis.

I still giggle about one time in particular. We both worked in the city and both commuted to and from work each day on our motorbikes. Every morning we would call each other to make sure that we had arrived safely – this was prior to smart phones and the tracking apps. This one morning I completely forgot to call him. I got to my desk and was immediately distracted by some urgent emails that needed attention. I then had a super-productive start to the morning and when he finally called I was feeling pretty good about my level of productivity.

As soon as I picked the phone up, he asked me how my morning was going – to which I responded, 'Oh, I hit the ground running this morning!' My husband responded with a shocked and concerned, 'Oh no! Are you okay? Did you hurt yourself?' It took me a few seconds to realise that he'd taken my response literally and thought I had actually hit the ground while I was running.

I laughed, maybe a little bit too loud, too hard and for too long, at the phrase I'd used so automatically and without a single thought about how it may be received. Of course, this phrase is used in other countries as well, but it was the first time my husband had heard it. Again, this is just one example of the many times the words I've used have created confusion.

Some of the other Australian sayings that are used without too much thought, and what they actually mean, include:

- 'Fair go' – used when someone feels like they're not being treated fairly.

- 'No worries' – everything is good.
- 'Dog's breakfast' – whatever is being referred to is a shambles or a complete mess.
- 'It's as useful as a chocolate tea pot' – it is completely useless.
- 'Better than a smack in the head' – things could be worse.
- 'Buckley's chance' – something is highly unlikely to happen.
- 'Pull the wool over your eyes' – mislead you in some way or evade the truth.
- 'Pull your head in' – stop being reckless.
- 'Put a sock in it' – stop speaking.
- 'Six of one, half a dozen of the other' – the outcome is likely to be the same whichever way you approach it.
- 'Get onya bike' – suggestion to leave or a challenge to the validity of what is being said.
- 'Hangry' – anger that surfaces over something small when you haven't eaten and are hungry.

Acronyms and initialisms

An initialism is the abbreviation of a number of words to just the first letter of each. For example, ETA is the initialism for estimated time of arrival. Others are likely to be equally as well known to you, such as COB (close of business), ROI (return on investment), and PTO (please turn over), used when a handwritten letter continued onto another page. An acronym is where this shortened form is pronounced as one word (rather than the letters separately), such as AIDS or RAM. But that in itself is getting complicated, so from now on I refer to both types as acronyms.

The danger of acronyms is that they can mean different things to people in different countries, industries, businesses and even across teams. For example, FTE stands for full-time equivalent in many corporate organisations, and relates to how many staff you have working for you according to a full-time person's hours (37.5 hours per week) instead of just headcount. So you may have four people in your team, but your FTE is three because two of your staff work part-time.

When I did some work for a not-for-profit, however, the acronym they used for the same thing is EFT, which stands for equivalent of full-time. For me, though, coming from banking, EFT stands for electronic funds transfer. So the conversation was all kinds of strange until I realised I had a different meaning for their acronym.

One of the things I encourage leaders to do is ask upfront what an acronym means to the person using it. You should also make a point of clarifying the meaning behind an acronym when you're using it. This will avoid any initial confusion and save time in the conversation.

How we perceive the world through our senses

The final point on words is that certain words will resonate more deeply for some people than others. Creating awareness around a person's preferences and using more of the words that resonate with them can also remove obstacles and build rapport.

How we perceive the world will be based on our preference for taking in information. We absorb information through our six senses: visual (what we see), auditory (what we hear), kinaesthetic (what we feel), auditory digital (what we tell ourselves), olfactory (what we smell), and, gustatory (what we taste).

Mostly we consume information from other people through just four of the six senses – that is, our visual, auditory, kinaesthetic and auditory senses. And of these we will have a preference for just one over the others.

Let's look at these four in more detail.

Visual

If my preference is to consume information through what I see and through pictures (moving or still, real or imagined), I will automatically use words that align with a visual preference. These can be words such as:

appearance	illusion	reflect
blank	illustrate	reveal
brilliant	imagination	scene
clarify	insight	see
colourful	look	shine
dark	mirror	show
dim	notice	sparkle
examine	obscure	spotlight
eye	outlook	survey
focus	overshadow	vision
foresee	overview	visualise
glimpse	perspective	vivid
hazy	picture	watch
highlight	preview	

As a visual communicator, I would prefer to learn through watching and seeing how things are done. Videos and people drawing diagrams, for example, will have a positive impact.

Auditory

If my preference is to consume information through what I hear and the surrounding sounds, I will automatically gravitate to using auditory words, such as:

accent	growl	ring
acoustic	harmonious	rumble
ask	harmony	say
audible	hum	shout
buzz	hush	shrill
cackle	listen	sigh
call	loud	silence
clear	melodious	sound
click	monotonous	speechless
comment	musical	squeak
croak	mute	tell
cry	pitch	tone
deaf	proclaim	tune
dialogue	question	vocal
discuss	quiet	whine
dissonant	remark	whisper
dumb	resonate	
echo	rhythm	

I would prefer to learn through listening and hearing instruction. Audio books and podcasts will be a key source of information.

Kinaesthetic

If my preference is to consume information through what I feel and experience, my automatic preference will be to kinaesthetic words, such as:

balance
break
cold
concrete
contact
feel
firm
gentle
grab
grasp
handle
hard
heavy
hit
hold
hot
jump
pressure
push
rough
rub
run
scrape
seize
sensitive
sharp
smooth
soft
solid
sticky
stress
stuck
suffer
tackle
tangible
tap
tension
tickle
tight
touch
vibrate
walk
warm

I would prefer to learn through doing it myself and walking through each step to get a feel for the process. Interactive training programs and simulations will work best.

Auditory digital

Finally, if my preference is to consume information through either visual, auditory or kinaesthetic and then follow this up with internal dialogue or self-talk, my automatic preference will be for auditory digital words, such as:

assume
attend
change
choose
competence
condition
connection
conscious
consequence
consider
decide
evaluate
future
goal
idea
know
learn
logic
meditate
memory
model

motivate	recognise	theory
outcome	remember	thing
past	representation	think
present	resource	understand
process	result	
program	sequence	

I will learn best if it makes sense, so explaining things in a structured, logical and rational way will work best.

Using perception in communication

If you can adapt your language to use the words that your listeners prefer, they will feel more comfortable with what you're saying and will absorb information quicker.

To start thinking about how you can make these tweaks, all you need to do is begin to notice what words the people you're talking with are using, and use them yourself. If they say something like, 'Yes, I like the sound of that', you might respond with something like, 'Great! Would you like to hear more?' You would have less impact if you said, 'Great! Would you like to see more?' because that's not their main preference.

So remember – words may only be 7 per cent of your total communication, but it's a very important 7 per cent that I think we need to take a little more notice of.

Tonality

Alongside words, and still aligned with verbal communication, is 'how' we say something – that is, our tonality. Tonality makes up 38 per cent of communication, so holds a lot of weight. It includes things like:

- *Pitch:* How high or low the pitch of the voice is.

- *Timbre:* The quality, or resonance, of the voice (for example, raspy, clean or crisp).
- *Tempo:* How quickly or slowly the words are spoken.
- *Cadence:* The modulation or inflection of the voice.
- *Content chunks:* How much is said between breaths and where in the sentence the pauses fall.
- *Volume:* How loudly or softly the words are spoken.
- *Rhythm:* Whether a monotone or a sing-song voice is used.

Tonality is often what makes the difference between someone perceiving a message positively or negatively. This means I could say exactly the same thing in two different ways and give what I say two different meanings. For example, I could say, 'You look great in that outfit', in a sing-song voice and with an inflection on the words 'great' and 'outfit', this would imply a compliment. Said with a monotone voice and without any inflection, however, would imply sarcasm and insult. The tone is the only thing to change yet what was first perceived as a compliment can easily become an insult.

As the saying goes, 'it's not just what you say but how you say it'. Consider how altering each of the components of tonality can affect how a message is perceived.

Non-verbal communication

With verbal and tonal communication making up 45 per cent, the remainder of what we communicate is made up of non-verbal communication – or our body language – at 55 per cent. It is through our movement and gestures that we share most about how we're feeling, our level of engagement and how confident we are with a person or on a topic. Indeed, we can actually communicate with someone without using verbal communication at all – and I'm not referring to sign language but to gestures alone.

During my travels through Europe in 2002 (before smart phones), I stayed in a remote part of Croatia with my Australian cousins and their Croatian Aunt and Uncle. We were there for about a week; we didn't speak Croatian and they didn't speak English. When we wanted something, we would gesture or point and they would do the same in return. It felt like a really long game of charades. They didn't have plumbing in their house so we had to learn where the water was for drinking, for filling the bath and for flushing the toilet but that was easy enough to communicate without words; it just took a lot longer. We ate what was put in front of us and were given home-made alcohol with every meal (including breakfast). It was very hard (although not impossible) to decline something using body language alone and not offend so we avoided doing that wherever possible. On the odd occasion, when we had a specific need, my cousins would call their dad who would translate for us. The time I spent there was relaxing and easy. It's interesting to reflect on the complication that verbal communication adds and how effective non-verbal communication can be.

So, if we're going to treat people the way *they* want to be treated, we should learn some of the components that make up non-verbal communication. These include:

- *Posture:* Whether you stand/sit tall and erect or with a curve in your spine. Whether your shoulders are back or rounded and whether you're leaning forward, back or sideways.

- *Arm position:* Whether you're standing with your arms crossed, by your side, in your pockets or on your hips.
- *Hand gestures:* How expansively you move your hands, including how rapidly and in what direction.
- *Head position:* Whether your head is tilted, turned or straight. When you're really engaged in conversation, you likely turn your head slightly to the side and tilt one ear towards the person's mouth so as to not miss a word.
- *Eye contact:* Whether you look the other person in the eye or avoid it completely, how long you hold the gaze and how often you do it.
- *Facial expression:* Whether you are animated, frowning or smiling (showing teeth or not) and any particular gestures.
- *Breathing:* Whether you breathe from the top of your lungs in the middle of your chest or from your belly. Remember that your breathing often aligns with your senses. People who have a visual preference will tend to breathe from the top of their lungs and quite quickly, and will also speak quite fast. Those with an auditory preference tend to breathe from the middle of their chest and don't speak as rapidly as visual people. Kinaesthetic people tend to breathe from their bellies and speak a lot slower than the other two types.
- *Muscles:* Whether you tense or relax your muscles, especially your jaw muscles.
- *Movement:* Whether you move a lot or not much at all, and whether your movement is fast or slow.

- *Skin complexion:* Whether the colour of your complexion changes. For example, if my face starts to turn red, this is generally an indication that I have said or done something that has embarrassed me, or that the temperature in the room has suddenly soared; unfortunately, it's generally the former.
- *Personal space:* The distance you're standing from another person when in conversation. Personal space will vary depending on the type of relationship you have with the other person as well as cultural factors and demographics. Growing up on a farm, my personal space used to be quite large, because there was room for it. When I moved to the city, it took me a while to get used to riding on packed trams and trains where personal space was non-existent – and no-one seemed too bothered by it.

When I coach leaders who want to be more effective communicators, much of the feedback I give is around what I'm observing in their body language. I talk to them about the intensity and grip of their handshake, how they're sitting in their chair and how their posture changes when they are feeling pressure or discomfort. Often the leader is completely unaware of changes in their body language and how others may perceive the changes. Non-verbal communication is one of our bigger blind spots, so my role as coach is to simply shine a light on it so they can work on making the necessary adjustments.

So what's my main advice around non-verbal communication? Firstly, there is no right or wrong way to sit, stand or move – it is all dependent on the context and the relationship that you have with the other person. It is important to calibrate on body language and how it changes throughout an interaction.

Imagine when a person first walks into a room that you take a still picture in your mind. In this picture you would capture the elements already mentioned, such as their handshake, their posture, speed of movement and eye contact. Then, as the interaction evolves, notice what has changed in comparison to the picture you took. And ask yourself whether this change is aligned with what you would expect given the type of conversation you're having. If it is, keep going. If not – their body language seems defensive or hostile, for example – make some adjustments, either verbally or non-verbally, to reconnect.

Here are two scenarios to show how body language might change throughout an interaction.

Scenario one

Eliza walks into your office. You notice that her head is held high, and her arms are swaying from side to side. Her body is open, her complexion is neutral; she's smiling and making a lot of eye contact. Her breathing is soft and normal.

The conversation you're about to have with Eliza is about concerns you have with her performance. You begin the conversation by asking how her day is going and then ask about her workload. As you do this you notice her arms cross, but you keep going. You ask her about her performance and how she thinks she's doing. You ask her what changes need to be made for her to succeed. You ask her what might be the impact of not changing. You notice that she has started to avoid making eye contact and her complexion has changed, her cheeks are now red. You maintain your approach and continue to ask questions and offer support where needed.

You are not trying to make Eliza feel better at this point, even though the caring, nurturing side of you wants to make the discomfort go away. It is in discomfort that we can learn the most, our brain is engaged and we're highly aware of the conversation. We are in the learning zone!

The conversation ends and Eliza leaves the room. Her pace is now a lot slower, she is a little slouched and her eyes are looking to the ground with her head lowered and her hands in her pockets. Given the purpose of the conversation, Eliza's body language has aligned with the desired outcome, which is to get her thinking and encourage her to make the required changes.

This conversation alone should not have any impact on your relationship with her, provided you're aware of your own body language and can slightly adjust to match. How you approached this interaction with Eliza isn't representative of all the interactions but purely built around the context of the conversation.

Scenario two

Tom walks into your office. You notice he is walking with caution and, as he enters the room, he hesitates slightly. His eye movement is from side to side and his breathing seems to be from the middle of his chest. His hands are in his pockets and his jaw muscles are tense.

The purpose of your conversation with Tom is to get to know him and increase the level of trust between the two of you. You are new to the team and have struggled to connect with Tom since coming on board. You decide the office isn't the best environment to have a conversation with Tom so you suggest going for a walk. You exit the building and head to the park down the street. You ask Tom about his weekend and what he does in his spare time. You ask how he is enjoying his role and what he did prior to coming to this organisation.

You notice as you're walking that Tom's posture starts to relax; his breathing moves to his belly and he is looking up more than he is side to side. Tom's hands are no longer in his pockets but loosely hanging by his side. The tension in his jaw has disappeared.

No actions are required at the end of this meeting; it has purely been one of relationship building. Tom leaves you at the elevator and you watch as he walks with confidence back to his desk, even cracking a joke with some of his peers on the way.

You can assume that this conversation has been equally as effective as the conversation with Eliza. Tom's body language didn't change quite as much but the intention of both conversations was fulfilled. It is body language that indicates the most about how a person might be feeling and what they might be thinking, but it's dependent on you as the leader calibrating as the conversation develops and being aware of the context.

Remember that increasing your awareness about someone else's non-verbal communication is just as important as becoming aware of your own. What message are you sending without even knowing it? Is your body language saying, 'I don't like you' while verbally you're saying, 'I really appreciate the work you're doing'?

What are you doing unconsciously that might be affecting your effectiveness and how might you bring your attention to it? If you don't already have someone who can help you with this, I would highly recommend pausing your reading here and going to find someone. It could be a coach or you might get a mentor or ask for feedback from a peer.

Your intention is to ensure your verbal and non-verbal communications are aligned so the message you're sending is as close as possible to the one being received.

Written communication

Separate from face-to-face or over the phone communication, written communication is mostly about the words we use. Tonality, volume, rhythm and pace cannot be heard or seen, only assumed. So getting the words, grammar and punctuation right is key to effective written communication.

Written communication refers to emails, text messages, messages sent via chat, and, of course, letters for those who still manage to put pen to paper. For the purpose of keeping this section of the book short, I'm only going to cover emails, because this is the most common form of written communication across businesses.

Of the leaders that I have worked with, both as an employee and in a coaching capacity, many are dysfunctional when it comes to composing emails. In fact, I have come up with three types of dysfunctional email communicators:

1. *The Dumper:* This is the leader who writes what they're thinking and/or feeling without any structure or clear objective. To make any sense of these emails, you must read them out and listen for the implied message – and you'll still probably get it wrong.

2. *The Fast and Furious:* This is the leader who writes in a big hurry. They need to get their message across as quickly as possible so their emails are often just one or two sentences. These emails lack context and are easily misunderstood.

3. *The Novelist:* This is the leader who writes about every aspect of the message they're trying to convey and goes deep into the detail. These emails are a massive data dump and include long sentences and slabs of text.

> The best way to make sense of these emails is to print them out, grab a highlighter, a crochet rug and a cup of hot chocolate and settle in for the afternoon. (These leaders may not have heard of Mark Twain's quote: 'I didn't have time to write a short letter, so I wrote a long one instead.')

Now, if you don't see yourself fitting into any of the preceding categories, chances are you're a good communicator ... and you're picking out the things wrong with the format and grammar in this book (which is okay and I'm happy to take feedback).

But if you do relate to any of these communication styles, you're not alone. In his book *Words that Work*, Dr Frank Luntz says that 'flawed language habits are so widespread that we encounter misunderstandings in everything from politics to business to everyday life'. And leaders have a lot to answer for when it comes to flawed written communication.

I have witnessed many disagreements in the past that have been the result of ineffective communication and, particularly, poor written communication. From yearly engagement surveys, you no doubt know that employees are constantly frustrated by confusing or unclear communication. And, as mentioned earlier in the book, most businesses solve this by setting up working groups to create more of it. We publish newsletters and updates, and provide regular messages from the CEO, which are all great ... but missing the point!

What we need to do is look at the quality of our communication, rather than the quantity, and work on improving it over time.

Clarifying your message

I've put together a few basic tips to creating a clear, concise message that will improve the engagement you have with your reader. The areas to focus on, and my tips for each of these areas, are as follows:

- *Subject:* Tell the reader what your email is about and what they need to do with it – for example, 'Action Required: New training module for frontline staff'.
- *Message:* Share the purpose of your email clearly. Make sure this is expressed in one sentence and position it at the beginning of the email. For example, 'This email is to let you know about a new training module that has been created as part of recent changes to legislation.'
- *Objective:* What do you want the outcome of your email to be? Include this as the next sentence after your purpose sentence. If actions are required, provide a timeframe for completion (or the actions won't happen). For example, 'Could you please read the information below and complete the required actions before 12 August?'
- *Language:* Keep it simple (year 9 equivalent) and avoid corporate jargon.
- *Audience:* Consider what level your audience is within the organisation. This will give you an idea on what background knowledge they have and what amount/type of information will be relevant.
- *Structure:* Break up the text by using headings, bullet points and numbers so it's easy to follow. Keep your sentences short and make only one point per sentence.

- *Personal:* Include a pleasantry at the beginning and/or end to let your reader know you care about them too – for example, 'I hope you're having a wonderful Friday!'
- *Review:* Finally, read, adjust and finesse your email before you send it out.

Let's look at a before and after example using this format.

Before

Subject: Blank

Hi Sandra,

As per email yesterday can you please advise if approval can be granted for Friday ?

Aside, in relation to theft of Thomas's mobile phone from his office, the appointment araged by the police last week to talk to him is tomorrow an they will be attending our office.

With this in mind the staff are constanly weary of customers calling in with pack packs an caps and viewing the cctv, is there anything you suggest I need to do for tomorrow i.e. be in the office.

With Thomas?

Your thoughts

Regards

Kate

After – broken into two separate emails

Email one

Subject: Approval required

Hi Sandra,

I hope you're having a great morning!

Following our conversation in yesterday's management meeting, could you please approve the below leave for James by **close of business today**?

Dates: Friday January 15th

Type: Annual leave – paid

Cover: The start and finish times for our two casual staff will be adjusted over this period to cover James's absence.

Regards

Kate

Email two

Subject: Update on mobile phone theft

Hi Sandra,

Me again!

Here is an update on the theft of Thomas's mobile phone from his office last week:

- An appointment for tomorrow has been arranged to speak with the police. They will be coming to our office.
- Staff are more vigilant of customers coming in with back packs and baseball caps.
- CCTV is being reviewed on a regular basis to look for unnatural behaviour.

Is there anything else you suggest I prepare for tomorrow?
Do you think I should be in the office with Thomas as support?

Regards

Kate

As you can see, by just changing the format and using clear and concise language, you can drastically improve the quality of your emails. Your staff shouldn't need to spend time deciphering messages or trying to figure out the purpose of an email; it should be easy and quick to understand.

Written communication isn't something that we become good at overnight. I am still on a journey of improving my own communication. I like to think that I have come a long way since writing my first book to the writing of my second. I also think I have more to learn and am constantly looking for opportunities to improve and seek feedback.

Building relationships and improving feedback

Written communication is also a great place for leaders to start when building relationships with their staff and providing feedback. I remember one leader I was coaching who had withdrawn from her peers and believed they were conspiring to get rid of her. She was operating from a position of fear but wasn't consciously aware of how her own behaviours were contributing to her performance and success in her role.

The organisation this leader worked for asked me to spend some time coaching her. When she agreed to work with me, I asked her what she would like to work on over the next six months. Her response was, 'Actually, Shelley, I think everything is going okay. I'm not really sure I need any help. I guess you could start by helping me with my emails!'

While it wasn't the response I'd expected, I took it as an opportunity to build some trust and raise the awareness this leader had of herself. I asked to read a sample email from her and then gave her honest feedback: I didn't understand what the point of the email was at all. I then asked her what her purpose was when sending the email, and to consider how the reader might perceive it and whether they would bother trying to make sense of it or just ignore it. I then asked what she might change to clarify her message.

In that session and many others over the six months, I was able to use written communication to highlight leadership opportunities. I was also able to use this to give her the confidence to take control of her own career and focus on improving what was inside her span of control, as opposed to focusing on things she had no control over.

Her realisation of how her communication was impacting her success allowed the conversation to open up and she began to trust that I was invested 100 per cent in her success. She confided that she thought I'd been brought in to get rid of her and that she couldn't believe the person she'd become. It was through improving her written communication that doors began to reopen, and she was able to rediscover the fun, confident and successful person she once was.

As her email communication improved, so too did her relationships with her peers and her manager. She became willing to pick the phone up and have a conversation with her stakeholders and to share insights and offer help when it was needed.

When we can get our written communication right, we can almost guarantee that the message we're putting out will be as close as possible to the one that is received at the other end. Remember that improving how we communicate takes determination and perseverance but the rewards are well worth it. Why not make this your next 21-day challenge?!

Monthly one-on-one conversations

One of the best opportunities to ensure effective communication across your team is to have monthly one-on-one conversations with each of your staff.

I've had hundreds of conversations with leaders and I'm still surprised whenever I hear a leader tell me they don't hold these types of conversations with their staff. Some leaders don't know they should be doing it and others don't see the value so don't bother.

Other leaders are having one-on-one conversations but they're a waste of time. The leader speaks at the staff member for 30 to 45 minutes, during which time the staff member nods and feigns interest, and then the staff member returns to their desk. The leader ticks the box and doesn't give it another thought until the next conversation – and nothing changes! This is probably worse than not having them at all.

As we progress through this book, you'll come to understand all the reasons one-on-one conversations are your biggest opportunity and should be your highest priority. These conversations should be the one meeting that never gets moved – they are your sacred cow!

I want to share a conversation I had with a close friend, and one that is typical of other conversations I've had with this particular friend. He is a passionate person so you really get a clear idea of his feelings. My friend, I'll call him James, was on the verge of quitting his job. He wasn't bored or uninterested in what he was doing; in fact, he loved the idea that what he did genuinely made a difference in people's lives. He hadn't outgrown his role and his performance was above average. He is a subject matter expert and enjoyed the challenge of the role. The thing is, he didn't really want to quit – he just didn't know what else to do.

His problem? He believed his leader didn't care! His exact words were, 'My manager doesn't give a #%*!' Out of curiosity I asked, 'How do you know that? Did she tell you that directly?' He said 'I only ever see her when she needs something from me or if I've done something wrong. She increases my targets all the time and making herself look good is all she cares about. She doesn't give a damn about us!'

Over the next hour James shared all the frustrations he was feeling at work and they all came down to one thing: the lack of one-on-one time he was having with his manager. He only knew her from what he saw from a distance and how he experienced her brief, infrequent interactions with the team. In the 15 months he'd worked in her team he had only had two conversations with her – first about his probation ending and second about his annual performance, when she told him he was doing well. She did not mention any ongoing development or express curiosity about what he was interested in. She had no idea about the person he was, either inside or outside of work, and he knew nothing about her, except that she liked to go to the gym.

What's sad about James's situation is that, when he gets annoyed enough and quits his job, the business will lose a great employee – someone who is loyal, hard-working and passionate about people and making a difference. And his manager probably won't ever know that she was the reason he left!

One-on-one conversations, when run well, are the perfect opportunity to get to know your staff at a deeper level. It's one hour a month for each of your staff, and it's one of the best investments you can make as a leader.

Recognising a good one-on-one discussion

Before you launch in to your next one-on-one conversation, I want to clarify a few things about what good discussions are – and what they are not.

One-on-one discussions are *not:*

- run by you
- unscheduled/zero-notice conversations
- a way of staying in control of your team
- a random chat with a group of staff
- a conversation purely focused on performance metrics
- a time used to reprimand or punish staff
- a tick-the-box conversation
- a discussion where you dominate and your staff simply nod
- a 10-minute grilling once a week
- a swing past your staff member's desk and check-in at random occasions.

One-on-one discussions *are:*

- run by the staff member – yes, you need to schedule them but they will drive the conversation
- an opportunity for your staff to feel heard without the attention of their peers
- a time to talk about development and opportunities for growth
- a discovery session on how staff are motivated and what the future looks like

- a conversation that builds rapport and deepens the working relationship
- a meeting where the leader speaks only 20 per cent of the time and asks questions to fully understand what's going on for the staff member
- an opportunity to influence outcomes and drive results through well-intended questions
- held once a month (no more and no less) and for a minimum of 60 minutes
- scheduled in advance – so your staff can prepare.

If you're not sure how the conversation should run, the following provides a simple template I've given to staff in the past so they can prepare in advance.

Goal:		
What went well last month?	What didn't go well last month?	What's your focus for the month ahead?
Support required:		

Their goal could be work- or life-related but is longer term and something they're committed to achieving. It's a great way to connect and take a genuine interest in their development.

Then they can reflect on what's worked well, what hasn't worked so well and what will be focused on for the month ahead, which will include specific actions.

Finally, the support required is any help they need from you or anyone else to ensure they succeed in their role and, more broadly, their life.

It's a great template that gives the staff member the opportunity to prepare in advance and sets the intention for the conversation that, 'It's all about you, and this is your hour!'

Fortunately, James didn't quit his job, but his manager moved on and his new manager gave him the time he needed to feel like he mattered. That's what matters!

Some final points

When you pay attention to communication, your awareness increases – both of yourself and of others. And when your awareness increases, you can start to see how interactions play out at both the conscious and unconscious level.

You can pay attention to what's being said while at the same time being aware of what's not being said. You can see how adapting your style and approach to match the other person can alter outcomes. You can build better relationships and establish a deeper level of trust.

Remember: if you want to become an influential leader, treating others the way *they* want to be treated is the place to start.

One last tip: if you like using diagnostics and tools when learning new skills, one of the tools I use for improving communication is DISC. This is a behaviour assessment tool based on the DISC theory of psychologist William Moulton Marston, which centres on four main behaviour traits shown by people: Dominance (D), Influence (I), Steadiness (S), and Conscientiousness (C). Understanding these traits – including which ones relate to you more strongly and which ones your staff align with – can enhance your leadership skills.

If you haven't done a DISC assessment in the past and would like to complete one, or learn more about it, let me know and I can arrange a time to chat.

CHAPTER 6 UNDERPINNING THEME: TIME

Time has been the reason for things not getting done for as long as I can remember – both in my household growing up and in the workplace. How often do you use 'time' as your reason for not doing something? For example, 'I don't have time to go to the supermarket today so we'll order in tonight' or 'I didn't have time to work on the project this week; I'll do it next week'.

Although we feel like we never have enough time to do everything, we have enough to do the things that matter … so this chapter is all about helping you understand what matters to you as a leader and how to use your time effectively.

> *Time is really the only capital that any human being has, and the only thing he can't afford to lose.*
>
> **Thomas Edison**

As a married mother of three children, all under the age of 11, who has been running a successful business and household for the past four years, I understand how you use your time matters. I don't have a great deal of support in my business, and most of the work is done by me. I am responsible for the administrative tasks, I write all my newsletters, attend meetings, run coaching sessions, develop training programs, facilitate team days, and I travel…oh, the travel! My husband's family are in South Africa and mine are in country Victoria, so we also have minimal support with the kids. Most of the 'getting stuff done' relies on the two of us coordinating our time to make things work.

And yet, I have still found the time to write this book!

Some say I'm crazy and others ask me how I do it, so here's my secret: I am intentional about everything I do and I pay attention to what matters.

In the two years prior to publishing this book, I spent many months 'working on it'. Each morning I would say to myself, 'I'll do some work on my book tonight' and each night I would sit down, well intended, with my laptop open – and then proceed to distract myself with emails, social media updates, LinkedIn messages, administration tasks and a variety of other mind-numbing options. I wrote a blog each week that aligned with the content of the book but I never even opened the Scrivener (the book writing program)! And I did this night after night before realising, at that point, the book didn't matter enough. So I put it to one side and focused on the things that mattered most.

As my business evolved, so did my focus and my priorities. Getting the book written began to matter. So I adjusted my lifestyle to make sure I found the time to write without compromising the other things that matter to me, like family and relationships. For just over a month, I set my alarm to wake up at 4 am. By the time the rest of the family woke up, around 7 am, I was ready to shut my laptop down and enjoy the day with them. The only impact of my 4 am rise was by 8 pm I was tucked up in bed sound asleep, instead of sitting on the couch watching Netflix with my husband.

The other thing I did was download an app on my phone called Dictate, which allowed me to talk through the content of each chapter. The app would then convert my spoken words to words on the screen. So, when I was out walking or driving, I would use that time to talk through the upcoming content. Then from 4 am, all I was doing was refining, and adding content and references as needed.

And here you have it: one completed and published book!

The following sections in this chapter outline how focus, energy, prioritisation – and even procrastination – can provide opportunities to work smarter.

Prioritisation

As I covered earlier in the book, one of the biggest problems new leaders face is spending too much of their time reacting to situations and, therefore, struggling to get ahead – because they are constantly putting out fires and fixing things that are broken.

A lot of this boils down to what you focus on and how you prioritise your workload. To effectively prioritise, you must have a clear idea of the end goal you want to achieve. If you're a new leader, this will likely be meeting the objectives that have been set for the business at the beginning of the year. Without knowing what you're aiming for, it's very easy to become scattered in your approach and spend endless time working on tasks that won't deliver your team a long-term benefit, but will simply alleviate some immediate pressure.

The Eisenhower urgent/important matrix (introduced in chapter 2) is a really good tool to help you map out your day, week and month. Figure 6.1 outlines what this matrix might look like for a new leader.

Figure 6.1: The urgent/important matrix for new leaders

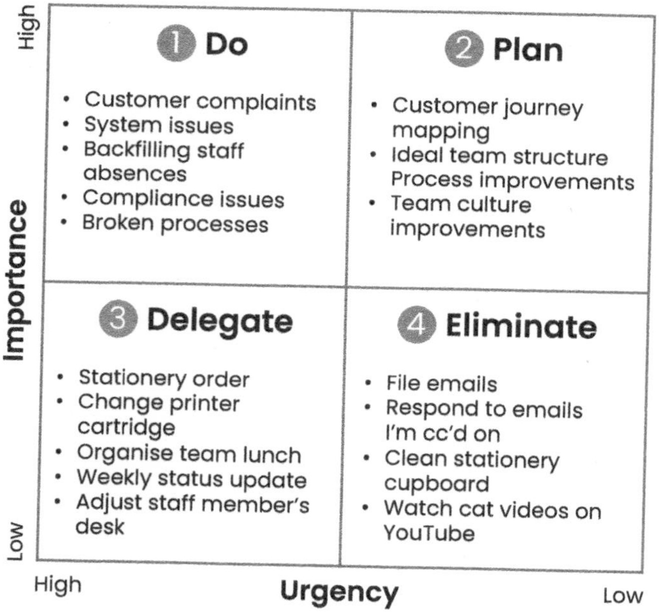

Perhaps the matrix shown in figure 6.1 is all you need to improve how you prioritise and manage your time. However, you need to find something that works for you, so allow me to share some further techniques that I've found really helpful throughout my leadership career.

Make the most of your mornings

Did you know that, on average, we make over 35,000 semi-conscious decisions every day? So, by 2 pm (depending on what time you wake up), you're starting to feel the effects of decision fatigue. That is why many experts suggest doing the most important things in the morning – because after lunch you're more likely to do what's easy over what's best.

So create a habit around making important decisions earlier in the day (for example, going to the gym) and trivial decisions later in the day (for example, what you're going to wear the following day).

Prioritise your to-do list

Some leaders love lists! To-do lists are a great way to get everything out of your head and onto paper. The process then opens up space for you to create or move to action on the important things. The challenge with to-do lists is many items are left un-actioned and over time this can lead to feelings of overwhelm and anxiety.

Here are some tips to help make your list work for you:

- Make a list of everything you need to do for the day or week.
- Add to the list any long-term actions you need to take to achieve your longer term objectives.
- Highlight all of the things that you enjoy doing.
- Underline all of the things you absolutely must do to succeed. (If you're not sure what success looks like in your role and/or life, pause here and seek clarification, either from your manager or a coach.)

- Rewrite the list in the following order:
    1. underlined/unhighlighted items
    2. underlined/highlighted items
    3. non-underlined/unhighlighted items.
- Indicate how long it will take to complete each item.
- Work through your list from top to bottom aiming to complete the task within the allocated time.

Your list might look a little like this:

- Customer complaints – 1 hour
- System issues – 30 mins
- Backfilling staff absences – 15 mins
- Compliance issues – 1 hour
- Process improvement – 4 hours
- Broken processes – 3 hours
- Customer journey mapping – 2 hours
- Team culture improvements – 1.5 hours
- Ideal team structure – 75 mins
- Stationery order – 20 mins
- Change printer cartridge – 10 mins
- Organise team lunch – 1 hour
- Weekly status update – 1.5 hours

Resist the temptation to complete the tasks that will take the shortest amount of time, particularly if they're at the bottom of your list. Start with the highest priority items and work your way down. Even if you only do the first 5 to 6 things on your list each day, you'll be making good progress over time.

Eat a frog for breakfast

This is one of my favourite tips and comes from the book *Eat That Frog* by Brian Tracy. Tracy has written over 50 books, consulted for more than 1,000 companies and addressed more than 5,000,000 people in over 70 countries worldwide – so he knows his stuff. 'Eating a frog' is the metaphor he uses for working on the one thing you've been avoiding – the thing you don't want to do but is absolutely essential for success. In the Eisenhower matrix, these would be the tasks in quadrant #2 ('Plan'). Tracy says:

> *If the first thing you do each morning is to eat a live frog, you can go through the day with the satisfaction of knowing that that is probably the worst thing that is going to happen to you all day long!*

If you can start every day eating just one frog, you'll be amazed at what you'll accomplish over a year. I've been using the concept for over seven years and can 100 per cent vouch for its effectiveness. The 1,000 words I forced myself to write every day, over 30 days, gave me this book.

Each night, set your 'frog' for the following morning. For example, 'Tomorrow morning I will brainstorm all the opportunities to improve our processes and then prioritise them' or 'I will complete the analysis for the business case I'm working on' or 'I will reconcile my accounts'. When you wake up or arrive at work, avoid becoming distracted by tasks that will take your attention away from eating your frog. For me, I avoid opening social media, emails or messenger.

Use your calendar

So many new leaders don't use their calendar, and most don't know they should. Or they'll use their calendar to accept invites to meetings they must attend but, aside from that, it just sits in the background.

Your calendar is one of your most precious resources when it comes to time management and prioritisation. I will often say to the people I work with that, 'if it's not in my calendar, it doesn't exist'. Rather than trying to remember who I need to talk to or who I'm due to catch up with, I'll put it in my calendar so it's out of my head and a time is scheduled for it.

I highly recommend you planning your time in advance – my calendar is constantly scheduled at least one month in advance, for example, and often also includes longer term dates for my strategic initiatives. I put things in there that I don't need to think about for a few months but will become important to focus on in time.

I also block out time to plan and create each week so I'm not always in meetings. This is a great way to set down what you'll focus on each day and so see how effectively you're using your time.

The more you use your calendar, the more accurate you'll become at scheduling the right amount of time for tasks and also challenging how long a meeting you've been invited to should take. If I've been invited to a two-hour project status update, for example, I'll ask which part of the update I need to attend and either go for the first or last half of the meeting. Other times, I will dial in from my phone so I can continue to work during the parts of the meeting that aren't relevant to me or my team.

If someone schedules an hour to catch up and provide a simple update on something, I know the meeting shouldn't take that long. So I ask them to reduce the meeting time to 15 or 30 minutes and to do it over the phone rather than face to face where possible. This stops commute time – even if it's in the same building, walking around an office can take up precious minutes of your day.

Some will recommend colour coding your calendar to highlight what kind of work you're spending your time on, but I think the first step is to just start using it!

Set a timer

This technique is really good if you have a greater focus on accuracy and getting things right, particularly when you have a deadline to meet. Consider setting a timer to give yourself a limit for how long you work on something. If you're not sure how long to set, use the Pomodoro Technique.

The Pomodoro Technique was developed by Italian Francesco Cirillo in the late 1980s. Essentially, you use a timer to break down work into 25-minute intervals. Each task is then separated by a short break (up to five minutes), before you start on the next 25-minute interval. (The technique is named after the tomato-shaped timer Cirillo used in university – 'pomodoro' is Italian for 'tomato'.)

When following this process, you set the timer for 25 minutes and, after the timer goes off, regardless of where you're up to in the task, you take a break. The break allows you to step back and make sure you're doing what's required to fulfil the requirements of the task. You then reset the timer for another 25 minutes and repeat until the task is complete.

Multipurpose your time

Multipurposing time is about fulfilling multiple objectives at the same time. For example, people who study and work full-time might conduct research while commuting to and from work – thus satisfying two objectives at the one time.

Look for ways to merge two tasks in your day-to-day routine – merging one that doesn't require a great deal of brain power (for example, commuting to and from work or exercising) with one that does (for example, learning new theory or creating content).

Here are a few 'multipurpose' activities you could try:

- listening to educational podcasts or returning phone calls while driving (safely, of course, and with a hands-free device)
- checking your social media while waiting for your morning coffee
- reading news articles while waiting for appointments
- improving your ability to read body language while attending meetings
- eating lunch with colleagues to strengthen relationships
- bringing your runners to work and holding walking meetings
- intentionally 'doing nothing' on your commute home to relax and unwind.

And a few for parents with young kids:

- feeding the kids while they're in the bath (it's amazing what they will eat when they're busy splashing about)
- getting your children to read to you while you're cooking dinner
- meditating with your children at bedtime (which doubles as 'cuddle time' along with your own way to relax)

- creating an adventure out of your trip to the supermarket
- folding the laundry while watching your favourite, pre-recorded TV show (... in fast play).

Follow the Pareto Principle

The Pareto Principle – or the 80/20 rule – put simply, is the theory that most of our results come from the least of our inputs. For example, 20 per cent of the work you do contributes to 80 per cent of your success. Or 20 per cent of your team will do 80 per cent of the work.

The Pareto Principle is good to keep in mind if you find yourself becoming fixated on getting something right when it just needs to get done, or getting something done when it needs to be right. You need to know what success looks like within the context of what you're working on.

Allow me to elaborate. By focusing on accuracy when accuracy isn't critical, you can miss immediate deadlines along with longer term opportunities. If meeting the deadline for a report was critical, checking it for spelling and grammar for the fourth time is career limiting – even if you thought that was an important component of the task.

Likewise, by focusing on action and getting things done when getting things right is more critical you're more likely to have to do the task over. Again, you'll limit your longer term opportunities. This is the case with any tasks around compliance or quality. Time isn't the key metric so your focus needs to shift.

So despite your preference for accuracy or action, remaining aware of the context and what is required to fulfil each task is really important.

The final point I want to make on prioritisation is that your priorities will change over time and as your career and life evolves.

Before children my priority was career progression along with health and fitness. I was in the gym five mornings a week by 6 am without exception. I was also known to still be at work at 8 pm. Now, my career is still important but progress looks different to what it did previously. And health and fitness have been de-prioritised by family and my relationship with my husband. Exercise now is often a walk or a hit of tennis with the boys.

So consider what your priorities are right now and revisit them regularly.

Focus

Based on the laws of attraction, what we focus on amplifies.

If I focus on all the things that are going wrong in my life, I inevitably attract more of it. In contrast, if I express gratitude and focus on all the things that are going well, I attract more good things. I've been living by this theory for the past ten years and it works, 100 per cent of the time.

So why are so many people focused on impossibility? Or on why things won't work? Some will hear others talk about amazing ideas and dreams but then counter this with myriad reasons why the ideas and dreams won't work, why we shouldn't follow them and why we should just be grateful for what we have.

This is one of the many challenges leaders must deal with on a day-to-day basis in the workplace. You might have staff who aren't open to pushing themselves and realising their true potential, or teams who don't want to adopt a new change, even when it will make their lives and jobs easier.

Or you might have an inner critic telling you you're in the wrong role and you're going to fail.

Rather than looking for what's possible, perhaps you find yourself (or members of your team) constantly gravitating to all the reasons why it's not. In thinking further about this tendency, I started to take notice of the things we say to ourselves – that is, the words that roll off our tongue so automatically that we don't realise their impact and what they attract as a result.

What I've started to notice is that our everyday vocabulary is often laced with statements of impossibility. Here are some I've observed:

- 'Don't get your hopes up.'
- 'Don't count your chickens before they hatch.'
- 'You can't have your cake and eat it too.'
- 'Let's not get ahead of ourselves.'
- 'You can't have it all.'
- 'With all great things come sacrifices.'
- 'Don't get your ambitions mixed up with your capabilities.'
- 'Never outshine your master.'
- 'You need to crawl before you can walk.'
- 'Where there's smoke, there's fire.'
- 'Your eyes are bigger than your belly.'
- 'Misery loves company.'
- 'It's like a red flag to a bull.'
- 'You're just asking for trouble.'
- 'It's all fun and games until someone gets hurt.'
- 'Just be grateful for what you have.'

And so on and so on …

And thinking back to my own childhood, I remember a 'Murphy's Law' poster that hung on the back of the toilet door – offering a list of sayings that were intended to bring light to unfortunate situations. The most popular version of Murphy's Law, of course, is, 'Anything that can go wrong, will go wrong'.

This fits in with others like:

- 'No good deed goes unpunished.'
- 'If you're feeling good, don't worry, you'll get over it.'
- 'Nature always sides with the hidden flaw.'
- 'Everyone has a scheme for getting rich that doesn't work.'

Oh, and my favourite: 'The chance of a piece of bread falling buttered side down is directly proportionate to the cost of the carpet.'

With ideas such as these that are simply part of our common language and outlook, it's no wonder our focus automatically gravitates to impossibility more than possibility. And this is such a waste of time – thinking about all the things that won't work or won't happen means that we're in exactly the same position as we started. We haven't made any progress, and often we've gone backwards.

To shift your focus, you need to start with your language – what you're saying and the words you're using. You need to comment on what is possible over what isn't. When someone asks you how you're doing, tell them you're awesome – even if you may not be to begin with.

Make a point of being that 'overly positive' leader until possibility becomes your default. Replace the kinds of phrases and comments I've already mentioned with new ones – for example:

- 'You can be whoever you want to be.'
- 'If at first you don't succeed, try, try, try again.'
- 'You are exactly where you're supposed to be right now.'
- 'Sing like no-one is listening, dance like no-one is watching and make every day count.'
- 'Life is what you make it.'
- 'Everything is awesome … everything is cool when you're part of a team … everything is awesome.' (Yep! You can even sing that one.)
- 'You have so much more to learn.'
- 'You're stronger than you know.'
- 'What did you learn today?'

No doubt you can think of the kinds of phrases and comments that work for you.

When we start to focus on possibility, we free up time and mental energy to try new things and work on the things that matter – like becoming a leader who staff want to follow.

Energy

In my earlier years, when I was fixated on health and fitness, I was given some simple advice: 'If you consume more calories than you use, the excess calories will be stored as fat. So calories consumed – calories burnt = calories stored.'

It was a simple concept that has stuck with me. The idea with weight is to consume the same or fewer calories than you burn each day to maintain a healthy weight range.

What's my point? Well, I see mental energy as being similar. If you receive more energy than you exert, the excess energy will be stored as mental fat. So energy consumed – energy burnt = energy stored!

The main difference between calories and energy is, to maintain a healthy mind, you need to consume more energy than you burn – that is, you need to have more mental fat!

So, how do you consume mental energy? Simple: do things you love to do. Even when you're exerting physical energy, some activities will replenish your mental energy – things like going for a run or a walk, or cooking, singing or dancing.

As a leader, it's helpful to know what activities or tasks give you energy and what take away energy. You could do this by going through your 'to-do' list and asking yourself whether you get satisfaction and energy from completing the task, or whether you feel bored, frustrated and drained of energy when doing it. Or, you may just start to notice what things you enjoy and how you feel afterwards.

When you have more mental energy, you're more inclined to work on the things that matter instead of just keeping busy. You become more effective in your role and as a leader. The key is to balance the tasks that burn mental energy with tasks that give you mental energy.

For example, I get energy from being around people, and particularly from speaking to people who have a common interest or a similar level or energy. So I'll make sure that I incorporate these kinds of conversations into my daily schedule.

I also know I burn a lot of mental energy when I have to sit in silence for long periods of time or do mundane admin tasks. So, on the days I need to complete these tasks, I make sure I end with a conversation with a colleague, listen to an inspiring podcast on the drive home or sing along to some upbeat music.

Knowing what gives you energy versus what takes it away will help you to plan out your week to ensure you're operating at your peak most of the time. If you know you have a whole day of tasks that don't give you energy, make sure you start and end your day with something that does. It's really important for your ongoing resilience to keep your mental energy levels in surplus.

The other impact on your mental energy and, therefore, your time is mindset – covered in the next section.

Mindset

Ever blamed something or someone when things haven't gone to plan? Does 'the dog ate my homework' excuse come up regularly in your workplace or household? How frustrating is it when you expect something to be complete by a certain time and find out it's not ready yet?

Or what about that conversation you have with another person when you run through all the things that are crap in your life and the constant problems you are facing. Perhaps you complain that 'luck' isn't on your side or ask why other people's lives are so good but yours isn't and 'it's just not fair'!

These are indicators of a 'reasons' mindset (see figure 6.2).

People with a 'reasons' mindset will often put the blame for something happening on someone or something outside themselves. They assume a victim role and, in effect, relinquish responsibility. Adopting a reasons mindset is easier than accepting you could be doing something differently. The problem with going through life with a reasons mindset is you have very little control over the direction your life is headed and, therefore, will likely not really move ahead at all.

Figure 6.2: A 'reasons' mindset

The good thing is that you have a choice. You can continue to have a 'reasons' mindset or you can decide to take control of your life and adopt a 'results' mindset (see figure 6.3).

Figure 6.3: A 'results' mindset

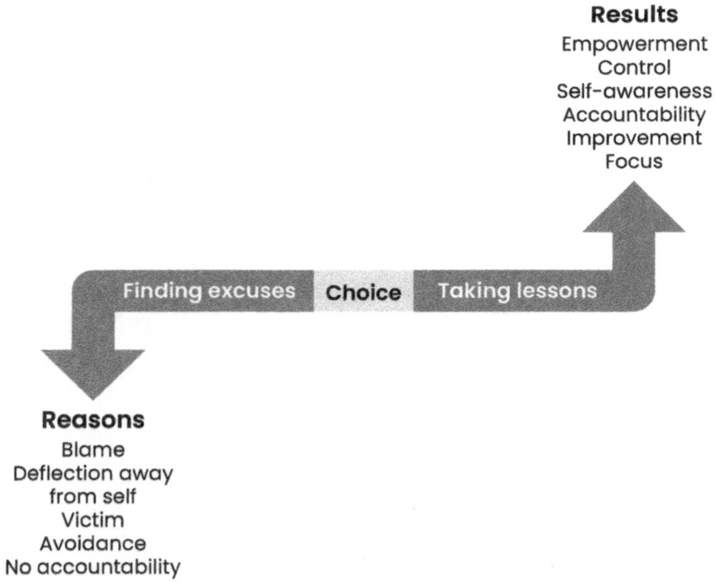

This 'results' mindset is what successful leaders adopt. They look for opportunities to do things better or differently. When they fail, they look for the lessons – rather than whose fault it was. They are clear on their direction and are in control of their future and what happens in their life – and in their business.

Adopting a results mindset isn't quick and easy; changing how you view situations takes awareness and perseverance. This mindset is, however, your longer term pathway to success. So if you can push through the initial discomfort, great rewards are at the other end.

The next time something doesn't go to plan:

- acknowledge what has happened
- ask yourself 'What could I do differently next time?'
- apply the lessons and commit to changing.

Here are a few examples to help you move from a reasons mindset to a results mindset.

Reasons mindset: instead of thinking …	Results mindset: consider …	Change required: take action …
The traffic made me late.	*I left the house later than I should have.*	Leave earlier next time.
No-one reminded me.	*I didn't set myself a reminder.*	Set a reminder in my diary.
They asked for this.	*I must have misunderstood what it was they wanted.*	Clarify my understanding with questions in future.
The dog ate my homework.	*I forgot to feed the dog so it starting eating paper.*	Feed the dog!

The better you become at managing your mindset, the better you'll become at managing your energy and how effectively you work.

Procrastination

I don't procrastinate over many things but when I do it's exhausting. I spend so much time getting the environment 'just right', I work on everything around what it is I'm supposed to be doing, and I allow even the smallest distractions to consume hours of my time. And when I'm not 'not working' on what I'm supposed to be doing, I'm thinking about it.

I see procrastination as a little like starting your car in the driveway but not going anywhere. The engine is running, you're using petrol and putting unnecessary strain on your engine, but you're not actually accomplishing anything!

Procrastination is probably one of the most frustrating things I experience and I'm guessing a lot of leaders feel the same.

So why do you (or your team) procrastinate in the first place? I've come up with three possible reasons and what you can do to overcome each of them.

Reason 1: You don't want to do it

We all have times when we need to do things that we don't want to. Perhaps the task is hard or monotonous or boring. In these instances, it's important to stay focused on the higher purpose behind doing this task. For example, if your higher purpose was to become a doctor so you could improve child survival rates in third world countries, you'd need to spend a number of years studying at university. You may not like the actual study but feel very strongly about being able to make such a significant difference in the world. So remaining focused on the higher purpose would be enough motivation for you to do the work and pass your subjects.

Daniel Pink, in his book *Drive*, calls this 'intrinsic motivation' – that is, the inner drive that motivates us to do things that don't have any material reward or an immediate consequence. When you can identify your intrinsic motivators, you'll find moving out of procrastination a lot easier.

Reason 2: You don't need to do it

If you're procrastinating over doing something that doesn't need to be done, simply decide not to do it. Remove it from your list and don't give it another thought.

If someone else has asked you to complete the task and you don't see what the purpose is, have a conversation with them about why they believe it needs to be done. (For further tips on having these kinds of conversations, see chapter 9.)

Reason 3: You don't know how to do it

Often when we're unsure of how to complete a task, we procrastinate over it. You may think you should know how to do it and are too proud or too embarrassed to ask, or you may not know who or how to ask for help.

If you're not doing something important because you don't know how, you need to talk to someone. You might just need to share your thoughts out loud for the task to start to make sense. A mentor is a great person to have in your network and perfect for talking to when you don't know how to do something. Alternatively, you could seek the support from one of your peers. Leadership is a learning journey and the path is well trodden, so don't feel like you need to go it alone and figure everything out yourself – many leaders before you have come up against a similar challenge.

Beating procrastination for good

So the three actions to take when procrastinating are:

1. Become clear on 'why' you're doing what you're doing – your higher purpose.
2. Decide whether to do it or not.
3. Talk to someone.

One final thing to overcoming procrastination is to allocate uninterrupted time to complete the task. If possible, allocate this time in the morning when you've got the energy and are less inclined to make excuses for not doing it.

Consider how, when, where, why and what you procrastinate over and work on getting your car out of your driveway!

Finding what works may require some trial and error so keep tweaking your approach until you find it – and then repeat this process whenever you're falling into procrastination mode.

Don't fritter your time away!

Time is one of our most precious resources, yet we use it like it's infinite. So much is wasted on doing things that don't need to be done, worrying about things that can't be changed and focusing on things for longer than we need to.

When a leader can manage their time, energy and focus effectively, everything else becomes easier. So figure out what approach works for you and apply a little discipline and determination to getting it right.

PART III
BECOMING A DYNAMIC LEADER

Throughout my working life I have experienced, first hand, what it's like to be a bad leader and a good leader. I have also worked under good and bad leaders. I have gained valuable skills and worked with experts in their field. I have trained alongside some amazing professionals, read countless books and absorbed as much information as I can about leadership and team culture.

What I have come to understand is there are three core components in becoming a dynamic leader and building a dynamic team. The three components are:

1. Investing in relationships
2. Inspiring respect
3. Influencing results.

What I see is that most new leaders focus on one over, and often to the detriment of, the other two.

At one end, you have leaders who place a high priority on people and tend to focus on building relationships with their team. They always have time for a conversation, never miss a one-on-one meeting and protect their team from the pressure to deliver. But this can also have negative effects. They often avoid having performance conversations and tolerate behaviours that negatively affect outcomes over time.

At the other end, you tend to have leaders who place a high priority on results and tend to focus on getting things done. They move with purpose and always appear busy. They don't pay too much attention to individuals unless it's regarding performance, and they are action-oriented. They often speak more than they listen and may struggle with high attrition and unplanned absences.

What leaders at both ends of the spectrum are missing is the ability to focus equally on both relationships and results. They can even swing between relationships and results, one day being supportive and nurturing and the next day bossy and direct. They don't have a balanced approach and staff struggle with their inconsistency.

The Dynamic Leadership model that I have designed and refined over the last few years has an equal focus on both relationships and results, along with what I see as the glue that holds the two together: respect.

Over the next few chapters in this part, we look at how relationships form the foundation of leadership and build trust. I then outline how respect deepens this trust and builds engagement, and finally how results are delivered through influence over power and control.

Woven through each of the three core components are the three levels of integration that will support leaders with their focus. The three levels are:

1. Say
2. Do
3. Be.

The following figure shows how my three core components and three levels of integration come together on the Dynamic Leadership model.

As you move through the model over the next few chapters, you can self-assess and identify opportunities for improvement. You may speed through some sections – those that are naturally inherent, for example – and take longer on others, and that is perfectly fine.

Figure 7.1: Three core components and three levels of integration

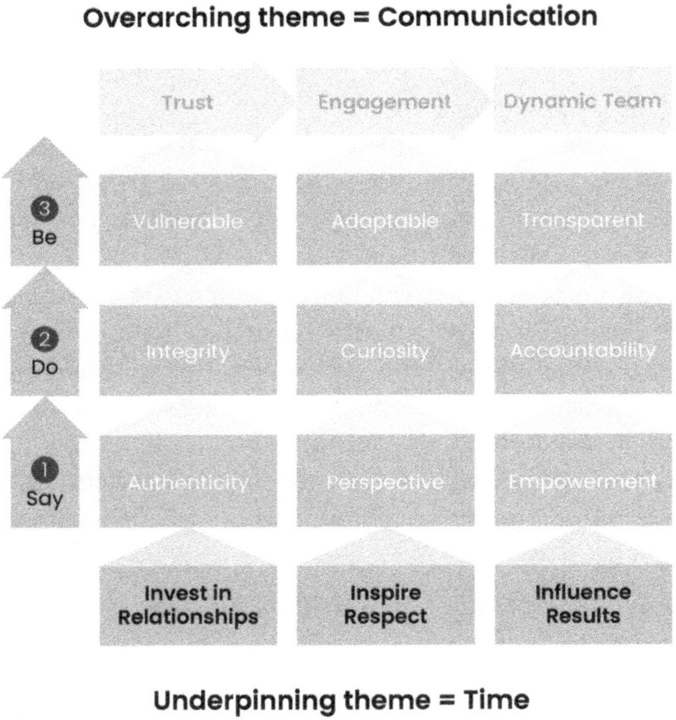

I would ask you to pause here for a moment and rate your ability as a leader. On a scale of 1 to 10 (with 1 being dysfunctional as a leader and 10 being dynamic), where are you right now?

1 2 3 4 5 6 7 8 9 10

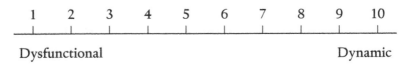

Dysfunctional — Dynamic

Consider what your intentions are for this book. What do you specifically want to get out of it and how will you apply the lessons learnt?

Once you've considered these things, you are ready to read on!

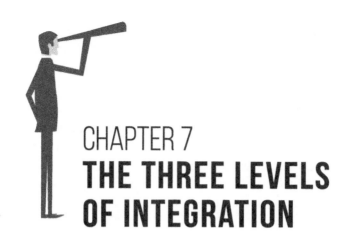

CHAPTER 7
THE THREE LEVELS OF INTEGRATION

The three levels of integration are the stages leaders progress through to achieve the best outcomes within each of the three core components of relationships, respect and results. The levels start with saying what you mean, then move to doing what you say, and finally focus on being who you uniquely are.

The following sections take you through the three levels so you can see how each is relevant and necessary for leaders to build dynamic team cultures.

Say

What we say matters! As we move through the three core components of relationships, respect and results, what we 'say' has a direct impact on how we are initially perceived by our team. It is what we 'say' that will form first impressions and determine how hard you'll need to work to gain and retain the trust of your team.

In your relationships as a leader what you say is about being authentic, saying what you mean and meaning what you say.

For respect, it's about offering perspective over opinion and asking more than you tell.

And for results, what you say is all about empowerment and how you go about enabling your people to make their own decisions and be their best.

Most relationships start with a conversation and many will end because of a conversation too so we mustn't underestimate the power of our words. Know that staff want to hear from a leader who cares, who inspires them and who believes in them.

Leading the way begins with what you say!

Do

As important as 'say' is for a leader, if they're not backing it up with what they 'do', it's a wasted effort. A leader who says one thing and does something completely different undermines and devalues any past effort. And similar to a business's reputation, a leader's takes time to build and can be undone in a single moment if they're not acting at all times with good intent.

'Do' for relationships is about integrity – doing what you say you are going to do and doing what is right. This means what's right not only for the leader themselves but also for their staff, for the business, for the organisation and for the broader community.

Do within the respect component is all about demonstrating curiosity. It's not just saying, 'I want to hear your opinion.' It's holding the silence long enough to hear and fully understand the other person's point of view, thoughts, ideas and contributions. It's listening with the intent to learn and not simply to respond. Curiosity is about removing judgement and being completely open to learning and understanding different ways of thinking.

And do for results is all about accountability. It is holding staff responsible for the commitments you have empowered them to make. It's doing it in a way that doesn't compromise the relationship you have built with them or the respect you've gained – your actions strengthen these relationships and respect. Accountability is holding not only your staff accountable for their commitments but also yourself accountable for your own commitments. It is putting your hand up and admitting your own faults and failures with your team.

So while what we say is really important, its effectiveness depends largely on what your staff see you doing and whether they believe this aligns with what you are saying. No longer is it okay to assume that people will do as you say and not as you do.

Be

The final level is 'be', and this is about consistency – how long, how well and how frequently you demonstrate who you are. Be is what determines the culture of the team. Be is what we say when we think no-one is listening and be is what we do when we believe that no-one is watching. Be is the level that many leaders fail to achieve because the components are often intangible and hard to measure.

Be for relationships is about a leader's ability to be vulnerable and have the courage to be imperfect. Vulnerability is about embracing your weaknesses and being okay with not knowing everything or always having the answers.

Be for respect is all about adaptability and understanding that the 'one-size-fits-all' approach doesn't work with dynamic leadership. Adaptability is being able to recognise what is needed for the individual, the situation and the environment, and acting in a way that delivers a positive outcome.

And be for results is about transparency – being completely open. While leaders may be unable to share certain aspects with their staff, other aspects that can be shared are often not. A transparent leader is open with their team and honest with information that they share. They aren't operating with a hidden agenda and don't feel like they need to withhold information to maintain power.

When leaders can operate effectively through all three levels of say, do and be, and are consistent in doing so, they will succeed. You will know when you've achieved success when you can spend a day or a week out of the business and the performance of your staff improves. They will be able to work autonomously and independently from you while still being able to support each other and keep the business running.

While 'say' and 'do' can be achieved by developing new habits, 'be' is about who you are and the culture of your team. 'Be' can only happen when 'say' and 'do' are aligned. When your team believes in their purpose and the contribution they're capable of making, they will become invested! So let's move to this important relationship with your staff and others in the next chapter.

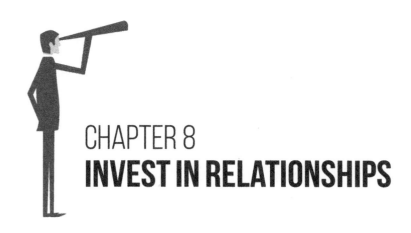

CHAPTER 8
INVEST IN RELATIONSHIPS

One of the biggest mistakes I made early in my leadership journey was thinking I couldn't be friends with my staff. I was told by other leaders (who I thought of as mentors) things like, 'You can't be too friendly with your people or they'll take advantage of you' and 'You need to let them know where they stand' – oh, and this one: 'Your team need to know who's boss; you can't cross that line.' All this advice meant the relationships I had taken months to form with my then-peers dissolved the minute I stepped into my first team leader role.

I cut myself off from the very people who could have supported me through a very tough, lonely transition into leadership. I have since, successfully, led teams where I have formed very solid friendships with my staff and delivered some terrific results.

It took me a while to come to this realisation but I no longer buy into the idea that you can't be friends with your staff. Having friends is often undervalued in leadership and, in fact, can make a huge difference to our energy levels, our confidence and our morale. According to philosopher Alain de

Botton (quoted by Poorna Bell in 'The History of Friendship' – see Sources at the back of the book for full details), 'We used to need friends for survival … now they are there to support us … the job has turned from physical to psychological.' You just need to be the friend who is clear on their boundaries, and be prepared to have the conversations that so many friendships are desperately lacking. You need to be authentic in what you say, show integrity in what you do, and be vulnerable. Figure 8.1 shows how all these relationship aspects come together to build trust in the Dynamic Leadership model.

Figure 8.1: The Dynamic Leadership model and the say, do, be of relationships

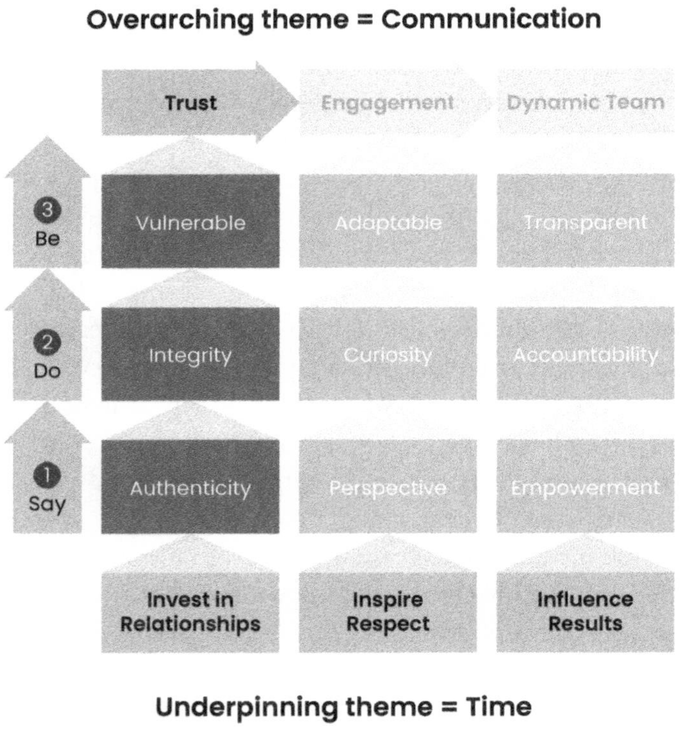

Working as friends and colleagues

I have heard a lot of reasons leaders think they shouldn't be friends with their staff but I've yet to find one that's valid. A lot of the time the reason comes down to a leader struggling to hold people accountable because of a fear of conflict. Or they believe that if they care too much about their staff, they'll become emotionally invested and won't be able to make rational decisions.

So rather than addressing the deeper issues around conflict and decision-making, leaders will simply disconnect and distance themselves from their staff.

To counter these fears, here's a list of reasons all leaders should become friends with their staff:

- Friends help you feel connected, like you are part of something.
- Friends care about you and if you care about the work you do, so will they!
- Friends want you to succeed.
- Friends have a deeper level of trust in you and vice versa.
- Friends have better conversations.
- Friends have fun – and we all know that time flies when you're having fun!
- Friends support you, particularly when you're going through a tough time.
- Friends help you expand your way of thinking by offering a different perspective or by sharing different experiences.

- Friends challenge you. A good friend won't buy into your bullshit, and instead will keep you thinking clear and focused on the bigger picture.
- Friends – real friends – don't take advantage of you! Karin Sieger, psychotherapist, says true friendships 'are based on unconditional concern for the other. We do things for the other out of friendship not in order to gain anything'. (Also quoted by Bell in 'The History of Friendship – see Sources.) If you have people in your life who take advantage of you, perhaps now is a good time to stop calling them a friend!

Some of the toughest and most valuable conversations I've had were with people I consider my friends. The lessons I learnt as a leader were invaluable and allowed me to become better and work through challenges with both compassion and logic.

Real-life example

I'll never forget a situation that occurred when I was leading a team of project managers and analysts. One of my staff members had successfully gained an opportunity in another team a month before Christmas. The role they were filling at the time was of high importance and couldn't be left vacant. So, rather than going through the formal hiring process, which would have taken two months (mainly because of the time of year), I took a shortcut by offering a six-month secondment for the position. This meant I could directly appoint and so didn't need to go through the whole recruitment process.

I knew the shortcut wasn't ideal but I was prepared to deal with the fallout later. So, not knowing anyone in my immediate team who would be interested in stepping into the role, I searched for someone in the broader business. I identified two team leaders who had a lot of potential and spoke with them both privately. One wasn't interested in the role but the other was. So after speaking with their manager, who agreed to release them quickly, the decision was made and I put out an announcement to my team.

Most of the team were happy with the decision I'd made and thought the new person in the team would fit right in. But there was one who didn't take it well at all. One morning, shortly after my arrival at work, he called me into a meeting room. For almost an hour he told me how unfair my decision was and how he had wanted to take on an opportunity like this and felt he'd been denied the privilege. I accepted everything he said and agreed to advertise and formally recruit for the role after the initial six-month time frame but for now my decision would stand. The meeting was great, and a lot of emotion was expressed from both sides. While I understood my staff member's point of view, however, I felt like he didn't understand mine.

Later that morning, I went for a walking meeting with my project manager, who was this particular staff member's line manager at the time. I shared what had happened to gain a different perspective and also keep them informed of what was going on with someone in their team. I said, 'I can't believe he reacted like that. I didn't even know he was interested in the role, it's really unprofessional to speak to me like that.' Okay, I went on for a bit but by this time I was frustrated and starting to rant.

My project manager turned to me and said, 'Shelley, you've built a team where you want people to be completely open and honest with you. That's what you got this morning! Someone trusted you enough to be upfront about his feelings and what he had perceived from the situation. That's a big deal and you can't hold that against him. You need to decide whether you want a team who will tell you how it is or a team who will just tell you what you want to hear! And you know what? He was right, the process wasn't fair. I get why you made the decision and I don't disagree, but you're just going to need to give him some time to work through it.'

To this day, that conversation remains one of the best I ever had as a leader. Everything that was said was true and it was me who needed to learn the lesson. It wasn't fair to appoint someone to the role, particularly without consulting my team, but it's a decision I would make again today. The lesson for me was the value of the friendships I'd formed in my team and honesty that came with it.

Nurturing any kind of relationship takes patience and perseverance. It's not always smooth and doesn't always feel good but if we can be friends with our staff, these conversations always seem to come from a better place. I know that my project manager cared for his people and I know he cared for me and the success of the team. While the conversation was really uncomfortable, I think if it hadn't occurred the discomfort would have been far greater.

As leaders we need friends who support us through our high highs and low lows. They are people who can call you on your bullshit when you start to wallow in self-pity and tell you when you've done the wrong thing.

The following sections of this chapter cover how leaders can really get the most of these friendships, investing in relationships through authenticity, integrity and vulnerability – to ultimately build trust.

Authenticity

authentic
adjective
1. Of undisputed origin and not a copy; genuine.

How nice is it to just be yourself? To speak freely, behave and dress as you like and do it all without worrying about what others may think.

Historically, this kind of freedom was limited to our life outside of work but we're now encouraged to embrace who we are – our uniqueness – and bring our 'whole' selves to work. That's nice, isn't it?!

But are they serious? Do the senior leaders in organisations really want all of their employees to be their authentic selves? Are they taking the lead and bringing their authentic selves to work each day? Do they even know who their authentic self is?

After spending most of my working life in the corporate environment, I feel like I'm still trying to figure out who my authentic self is! I think the biggest challenge leaders face is relearning something we've learnt to forget – to be authentic.

You see, I think authenticity is something we're born with and then we're taught to suppress and ignore it. Consider how many preschool aged children you know who aren't authentic. My three year old is an open book: she'll tell you how she's feeling and what annoys her, and she'll sing and dance around the living room without a care in the world. She is influenced by her surroundings to a certain degree but, ultimately, she's just being her true authentic self (which is absolutely adorable, by the way).

Compare this to my older boys, who are now in grade 2 and 6. They have both become very guarded about their ideas and opinions. Since starting school, they have gradually built up their awareness and changed who they are – I assume in order to 'fit in'. It's no longer okay to kiss mum in public, for me to walk them to their classroom (they want me to leave them at the front gate of the school) or hold hands and skip through the park. They have, like many of us, conformed to the norms of society and the environment they live in.

I was no different when I was growing up. I was one of those kids who struggled to fit it, conscious my teeth were too big, my clothes were hand-me-downs and my parents drove a Kermit the frog green-coloured panel van – which you could see coming from about a kilometre away. I remember being the one other kids would pick on – if I wasn't being called 'Bugs Bunny' or 'ugly', they were laughing at the car I arrived in. The only way I knew to make it stop was to try to blend in, so I stopped smiling, so my teeth didn't stand out, I got a part-time job and saved all my money to buy brand-name clothes and, like many other kids, I walked where I could and got my parents to drop me off far enough away that no-one would see the car they drove. And I shut the lid on authenticity. I didn't want to be genuine; I just wanted to fit in.

I learnt to fit in, to co-exist and conform to certain societal norms. Now, after spending decades being someone who I thought others expected me to be, I'm still trying to figure out who my authentic self is.

Resisting pressures to conform and finding authenticity

Solomon Asch conducted an experiment in the 1950s as part of his study into conformity. The experiment was devised to examine the extent to which pressure from other people could affect one's perceptions. He found that around one-third of the subjects placed in this situation went along with the clearly incorrect majority. Asch was disturbed by the results and concluded 'the tendency to conformity in our society is so strong that reasonably intelligent and well-meaning young people are willing to call white black'.

What he found was that people conform for two main reasons: because they want to be liked by the group and because they believe the group is better informed than they are. (Saul McLeod provides more information on Asch's study in his article 'Solomon Asch – Conformity Experiment'; see Sources for full details.)

I concur that new leaders in particular believe in both of these reasons and I think this is one of the struggles they face – that is, they are torn between being liked and trusting the 'wisdom' of the group, and knowing they need to be authentic. What does it even look like for a new leader to be their authentic self and is that really who an organisation will embrace, promote and look to for inspiration?

To further blur the authenticity lines, a new leader will often start to walk, talk and dress the way they believe a leader should, and so give up what makes them who they genuinely are. And this doesn't go unnoticed by their staff, who start to see them as 'copycats'.

Embracing authenticity and bringing our 'whole self' to work is a gradual process and starts with working out who you are. What's important to you? What do you value? What are you not willing to compromise on?

Then it's a matter of opening up to your staff about who you are, both in and outside of work. You might share your career goals along with your hobbies and some of the experiences you're having with your children or pets. To build authenticity in your team, you will want your staff to feel like work is also a safe place for them to share and open up in.

And if you want your staff to be their whole selves, you need to be prepared to go their first.

In my Dynamic Leaders program, I talk about authenticity in terms of building relationships, and getting to know your people on both a work front as well as a personal one.

When a leader can embrace their true authentic self and do it in a way that continues to build confidence and maintain a positive environment, staff will follow their lead. Leaders not only need to embrace their true authentic self but also take a genuine interest in the authentic selves of their staff, their peers and even their own leaders.

Start with what you say

Developing an authentic connection with the people you work with starts with a conversation. This might be saying good morning to everyone when you come into work each day. Or it might be having casual and random conversations with your staff about things outside of work or other random topics. Small talk is a golden key for building relationships and opening up authentic conversations. Be prepared to have a conversation about any topic, even if you have no clue about it.

When you're encouraging others to open up and be their whole selves, you need to be able to share, without judgement, the activities of interest that you have in your life. Learning about your team will allow you to deepen the relationship you have with them. It will also give you an idea of what it is that motivates them.

If I know that a staff member is interested in working creatively in their spare time, I can make sure I give them the opportunity when it arises within the team. If we have an event that needs posters or flyers designed, for example, I'll know to go to them for help. Keeping track of these unique pieces of information about your staff can help to improve motivation and strengthen team culture. There's really nothing better than your leader remembering something important you've shared with them months earlier. It shows they genuinely care and have taken the time to understand you not only inside of work but outside too.

If you're like me and struggle to remember who said what, a simple tip is to keep a record – a little black book, for example, of the information you collect. Of course, I don't mean anything creepy! You wouldn't record anything confidential, but rather just random and open pieces of information. You might jot down information about your staff members' hobbies, sports they like, where they grew up, number of siblings, ethnic and religious backgrounds, goals and life dreams, and any other interests that they have discussed with you and that may come in handy.

So the key to authenticity is figuring out who you are as a leader and learning who your staff are as people. It is about providing a safe environment for everyone to be their 'whole selves' and taking a genuine interest in their lives. And, finally, authenticity is about saying what you mean and meaning what you say – which links in with the topic of the next section!

Integrity

> **integrity**
> *mass noun*
> 1. The quality of being honest and having strong moral principles.

Integrity, in my opinion, is doing what you say you're going to do and doing what is right. Not much bothers me more than a leader who says one thing and does something completely different. Or they say they will do something and then they don't.

I get that we are all human and sometimes we commit to things that we believe we'll follow through on but, for whatever reason, we don't. And if this happens on the rare occasion, usually no harm is done. When it becomes a regular pattern, however, it can severely affect your integrity. When, even before you commit to something, your staff know it won't get done, the impact is high.

Other leaders say yes because that's the quickest and easiest way to end a conversation. When they don't have time to go into detail or debate a topic, they will opt for saying yes in the moment and then seeking forgiveness for not acting after the fact.

Some leaders say yes because they don't want to make the other person feel bad or they don't want to cause any type of conflict. They will generally be quite overwhelmed with all the other tasks on their to-do list and will feel bad about not getting your thing done. But instead of having a conversation with you to realign expectation, they will avoid you for the next week or so until they think you may have forgotten about it.

Whatever the reason is for saying one thing and doing another, you must know that it compromises your integrity, regardless of what your intention is. And a leader without integrity isn't going to ever build a dynamic team. So if you're doing things that are compromising your integrity, stop it!

Recognise the importance of what you're saying yes to, make the commitment and hold yourself accountable (or ask others to hold you accountable). Be realistic about what you can do and what might need to wait (don't be afraid to say no if you don't have the capacity). And beware of the excuses that can easily roll off your tongue – such as, 'Something more important came up' or 'I ran out of time' or 'I completely forgot'.

> *Doing what you say you're going to do, because you said you would, is a pretty simple definition of integrity.*
>
> **Nate Zinn**

Aside from saying one thing and doing another, the following sections cover some other moments when your integrity, as a leader, could be compromised.

Meetings

You know that moment in meetings when a task needs an owner and the question is asked, 'Who wants to take this on?' How do you handle the silence that follows? If your discomfort with silence outweighs the reality of your workload, no doubt you put your hand up. And it's likely you leave the meeting with the most actions and the least time to complete them.

Team building and strategy days

Is there anything that annoys staff more than being pulled out of their day-to-day work to attend a 'team day'? The work keeps piling up while they're away, so when they return they have all these things to catch up on. Or perhaps they have made an investment in the design and shaping of something during a team building and strategy day, and ideas have been committed to and actions formed with timelines and so the day ends with much excitement and enthusiasm – only for staff to find that, when everyone returns to the workplace, nothing happens.

I have lost count of the number of 'team development days' I've attended where excitement is generated, ideas are created, actions documented and, then…nothing happens. Zero, nil, zip. I get frustrated just thinking about it, particularly when I consider what I could have been doing with the time I spent away from my own team. That initial feeling of excitement then turns to disappointment and often disengagement! If integration back into your workplace doesn't happen and nothing changes, staff will feel like their opinions don't matter. They can become unmotivated and old behaviours might amplify. The flow-on impacts can be a decline in productivity, performance and team morale. And, getting everyone together outside of the workplace becomes a complete waste of time, money and effort.

Venting

While venting is a natural and healthy process we go through to air our frustrations and release negative emotions, as a leader you must be really careful about how, where and with whom you do your venting. The worst way of venting is to turn to a staff member and blurt out what happened and how you feel about it, particularly if it has something to do with another staff member in your team or another team. The team member you're venting to in such a situation often doesn't have access to the same information as you and could take your comments as fact – which can create a fractured culture and resentment below the surface.

The best way of venting is to vent to yourself. I find typing a note (that can't be accidentally sent) outlining your frustrations and emotions to the person who has been responsible is a great way of 'getting it out'. You can then quickly delete the note so no-one ever sees it. The other option is to go for a walk outside and talk to yourself about what just happened – making sure no-one else is within earshot. Or you could vent in your car on the drive home, with music playing really loud and windows up so you can get rid of all the negative energy that's come and tire yourself out before you get home. Finally, you could vent to a person you know won't take sides and won't buy into your story, and will instead just listen and nod while you get it all out. These people are very hard to find but absolute gold when you do. They will never agree with what you're saying or contribute to the venting; they will just be there. Once you're done, they will forget they ever heard anything and will remain neutral – this is what makes them so hard to find. It's extremely hard to listen to someone's story, especially when that person is clearly in pain or discomfort, and not try to make things better or do something to help. It's what we're wired to do as humans. But when someone is venting we absolutely must never get involved. Venting happens when emotions have overridden logic, so often what's being said isn't realistic and the situation will be seen very differently in a few hours or days once the emotion subsides.

Gossiping

People will always talk about other people and, as a leader, you need to be able to navigate this sometimes dangerous area. Fine lines separate when you should engage with this talk, when you should intervene and when you should simply walk away. When someone is speaking about someone else with admiration and positive intent, usually no harm is done. When someone is speaking about someone else with a negative intent, however, or without having all the facts, this talk becomes gossip and needs to be stopped.

Gossip in a team erodes trust quicker than any other behaviour in the workplace. The lure of the juiciness of the conversation and the connection that is formed when you have a similar belief about another person or action can be so strong that many people don't have the willpower to resist it. While I discourage staff in general from engaging in pointless gossip, for leaders the effects can be especially negative. In fact, engaging in gossip as a leader is the best way to destroy your brand and lose credibility.

I really hate gossip. It's something most of us are first exposed to in primary school and I think it comes from the creative part of our brain – where we're given a few pieces of information and we allow ourselves to fill in the blanks, without any evidence of whether the version we create is true or not. Then we share this version with a friend, who thinks it's a great story and so shares it with their friend. Only they make their own adjustments, adding or changing some of the information, and so the story is shared from person to person morphing along the way and without anyone questioning the validity of the second-, third- and fourth-hand information. And because we learn to do this at such a young age, as adults, we do it so automatically that we're often not even considering the damage we might be doing to someone else.

If you've ever had someone gossip about you, you'll know firsthand how terrible it feels. It can not only erode your confidence but also cause unnecessary conflict with others. Gossip is one of the main reasons I left my country life and moved to the city. In the country, everyone knew everything about everyone – and when they didn't know, they would simply make it up. 'Oooh, there's Shelley's car parked outside John's house. I wonder what she's doing? I bet she's having an affair, do you think we should tell her boyfriend?!' And regardless of the reason my car was parked at John's house, my boyfriend would inevitably hear the gossip, we would argue, and often break up for a short period of time before making amends. It was the most frustrating experience!

Remember, as a leader, you are responsible for, first, resisting the temptation to get drawn into gossip and, second, shutting it down when you hear others engaging in it. It is toxic and can quickly spread if not contained.

Corridor conversations

A 'corridor conversation' is an informal meeting that happens after a formal meeting. It is usually between two or more people who have attended the meeting and gather in the hallway on their way back to their desks, and is often used as an opportunity to voice honest opinions that have been withheld during the meeting itself. While corridor conversations can sometimes be helpful, offering different perspectives and helping you make better decisions, most of the time they're unproductive and not an effective use of time.

Corridor conversations often end up leading to venting or gossiping, so if you can avoid getting drawn in or drawing others in you will protect your integrity. If you've left a meeting feeling like you haven't been heard or you need clarification on a particular topic, it's your responsibility to meet with the appropriate people to resolve this issue, not complain to others who aren't in a position to make any difference.

When you notice your staff members engaging in these conversations, you might talk to them about the purpose of the conversation. Are they planning on taking any action as a result and is this the most effective use of their time? You might suggest the conversation take place with the relevant person or people, and ask how they might go about setting up that conversation. Keep your tone casual and light-hearted and pose questions rather than make commands. Staff can laugh the situation off, to avoid embarrassment with their peers, but will consider what you've asked and will likely take a different approach next time. Your observation of these conversations is also useful, so you may want to talk through things individually with staff in their one-on-one conversations. You may uncover underlying concerns or fears they may have about addressing the issue more directly, and you may be able to help them to work through it. Or you may simply challenge them on their behaviour and the impact these kinds of conversations might have on the culture of the business.

Inconsistent behaviour

Here I'm talking about the kind of person who says one thing *to* you and then something different *about* you. This really bothers me and I've never understood what reward comes from doing it – it really is schoolyard behaviour so doing it in the workplace is extremely immature. I remember working in a role where I sat directly opposite the head of the department in an open plan space. Why she didn't have her own office, I'll never know but she certainly needed one because she had no filter. I had spoken with her one on one a couple of times and got the impression that she cared and wanted to do what was right by people – that was until I overheard a conversation she had with one of her leaders.

I'll never forget listening to her speaking with this particular leader over the phone. While I didn't hear what was being said on the other end I could hear from the compassion in the head of department's voice that the person was going through a hard time and really needed support. I remember the head of department reassuring her and offering support as they worked through whatever the issue was. The conversation went on for about 45 minutes and sounded helpful and authentic. So I couldn't believe what I heard next – as soon as she put the phone down, she turned to her assistant and groaned. She then proceeded to berate the other leader and vent her annoyance at having her time wasted. She made comments around what she expected from her leaders and was pissed off that this leader needed so much attention when she should really 'just get over it'.

I honestly wish I had never overheard the conversation because I never felt the same about the head of department again. I would refuse to work with very few people, but there isn't enough money in the world to convince me to do any work with this person in the future … ever! Clearly for me this behaviour triggered a deep conflict in my values so I'm sure not everyone would have the same reaction, but be aware that there are certain actions that you may never recover from in your staff members' eyes – and, for me, this is one of them.

Deferring blame and assuming credit

Deferring blame is where you make everything about someone else when you should be looking at the role you've played. Deferring blame is pointing the finger and looking for excuses instead of learning from the situation. It is often referred to as 'throwing someone under the bus' and is a really quick way to lose the trust of your team. Similar to deferring blame is assuming credit for things you haven't had anything to do with instead of recognising your staff for the role they played.

The old cover up

This is pretending something didn't happen. I'm not sure I need to elaborate any more on this point. It's like a parent who watches their child break a plate and then asks, 'Did you break the plate?' – and the child refuses to admit to what they've done even though their parent watched the whole thing. I guess some kids get away with that for so long they carry it into adulthood!

Lack of follow-through on consequences

I'm talking here about when you warn or threaten a staff member with a consequence and then you don't actually enforce the consequence. Often this initial threat or warning is uncomfortable enough for the leader to never want to do again. So when the behaviour doesn't change and it's time for the consequence to be put in place, leaders get shy, make excuses and often go to some extreme measures to avoid following through. What this does is reinforce the negative behaviour, which continues to cause issues longer term.

According to speaker and author Brian Tracy (of *Eat that Frog* fame – refer to chapter 6):

> *Integrity is a state of mind and is not situational. If you compromise your integrity in small situations with little consequence, then it becomes very easy to compromise on the big situations.*

It's the little things you compromise on that send warning signals to those you deal with – telling them to be cautious about you and so eroding the trust you've worked hard to build.

Remember – your integrity is one of the most important things you have, so do what is right. If something doesn't feel right, chances are it probably isn't. Go with your gut. If you need an extra filter for this one, ask yourself whether whatever is being discussed is something you'd be happy to share with the world. If it's not, don't proceed.

Vulnerability

vulnerable
mass noun
1. The quality or state of being exposed to the possibility of being attacked or harmed, either physically or emotionally.

Remember being that little kid who did the wrong thing and had to 'own up' and apologise, while your parents looked down at you with complete disappointment? Do you remember that feeling of embarrassment and shame that made you feel so small you hoped the world would just swallow you up?

Moments like these – which we continue to experience throughout our childhood, in some form or another – teach us to build up layers of protection. These layers are formed to protect ourselves emotionally, from being embarrassed and feeling ashamed about something we've done. By adulthood, these layers can be protecting us from being exposed to any emotional discomfort. We might shut off our emotions and focus predominantly on thoughts. We might change the topic of conversation if it makes us feel uncomfortable. We might argue every little point in an attempt to retain control. We might turn serious conversations into jokes by using humour to lighten the situation. We might remain silent or become silent when we're feeling compromised. Or we might avoid situations where we'll look stupid.

Understanding your protective layers

Even if your protective strategies take a different shape than the preceding examples, you will have created layers upon layers throughout your life in an attempt to preserve your vulnerable self – we all do.

And now, here you are, in a leadership role, with everyone watching to see what you'll do. It feels like you're on centre stage and the crowd is urging you to expose yourself, to show them that you're human, but you're desperate to never feel like that 'naughty little child' ever again and so you remain hidden under all the layers you've built up throughout your life. So what do you do? Perhaps some of the following:

- You take things too seriously – so much so that you've lost your sense of humour, and the things that used to make you a fun person to be around.
- You refuse to make decisions – just in case they're the wrong ones – and so have built yourself a reputation for being a difficult stakeholder.
- You micromanage – because you are responsible for your team and they were once naughty little children too, so surely they can't be trusted.
- You hold on too tight – so tight that nothing moves, you start to stall, and become stagnant and stale in your career.
- You develop a FOMU – fear of messing up – and you start to second-guess everything you and your team do.

> As your FOMU increases, so too does the likelihood it will happen.

Before you know it, you've completely lost your identity and what makes you unique. You hold a belief that leaders need to be 'super-human' so you put pressure on yourself to know everything, to never admit to being wrong, to always have a solution and, above all, to never show emotion … all in an attempt to preserve your emotional self. Many leaders have gone through their careers like this, never really showing their true self, just allowing glimpses of a human-like figure hiding below the surface, scared that one day they'll be exposed. Their career will be tough and their automatic default will be one of defence and judgement, but, if they push hard enough, they might make it through.

In the 21st century, though, these leaders are exposed very quickly and are either forced to change or forced out. It is the leaders who can embrace vulnerability and their true sense of self who will succeed in today's world.

Allowing vulnerability

A leader who embraces vulnerability isn't afraid to say they don't know the answer. They don't profess to know everything and are the first to put their hand up and tell others when they've made a mistake. They talk about emotions and share the human side of themselves, even if this might mean others will judge. These kinds of leaders have the ability to demonstrate greater levels of compassion and empathy, and their staff can relate to them on a human level.

It is only when a leader embraces vulnerability that their staff will feel safe enough to go there too. If they see a leader sharing insecurities and apologising for something not going the way they first expected it would, they can also embrace that as a way of working, developing and constantly improving.

So, what do you need to do to show your team you're human, that you make mistakes, that you can learn from them and that you care? Simple: show them … go there first.

I feel like it's the right time in the book to be vulnerable myself. To share with you the most embarrassing, shameful experience I've ever had in my career. I want to share my story because I know many other leaders have been down a similar path and, hopefully, I can help those who are on the path now to make some changes to alter the outcome. I am sharing my story with complete awareness that some readers may judge me or think I'm not worthy to be writing this book. But I'm doing it anyway, because I want the world to know that I haven't got to where I am right now the easy way. I got a little dirty and roughed up along the way, but I came out a stronger, kinder person as a result. So if you must judge that's fine, just know that as you're judging me, someone out there is judging you!

Okay, here goes!

My leadership rock bottom

Just before I gave birth to my first child I took on a role that wasn't as stressful as team leading in the contact centre. I became a business analyst in a support function, which allowed me to step out of the running of the business and into the planning, strategic and improvement part. I had no direct reports and felt like I'd gone from drowning in an ocean of work and issues to relaxing in a bathtub. I was able to consolidate everything I'd learnt and start to see things from a different perspective. However, I also realised that I missed leading people and working in a fast-paced environment.

So when the opportunity came up in the same organisation to lead another team in a back office area soon after my son was born, I was excited and jumped in head first. This new team was completely unknown, and I went from being a subject matter expert to having zero expertise in what they did. I was immediately frowned upon. Comments from my team included, 'Who do you think you are coming into this team?', 'You have no idea what we do or how to manage us', 'They've made the wrong decision', and 'You won't be around long'. I don't recall these comments being hurtful – probably because of the protective layers I'd built – and instead I saw them as more of a challenge. The team had a very diverse tenure of people, with some having been there over 20 years and others just a few months, but even so there was a deeply embedded culture of 'their way of working' – combined with scepticism and distrust of this young new leader who'd just arrived. It's something that with hindsight I could have paid more attention to but I didn't; I just got on with my job.

Focusing on results and ignoring my team

The other thing I didn't pay enough attention to was that organisation-wide restructures meant some of the people who'd been there a long time were feeling hurt and unfairly treated, and this hadn't been addressed. After a number of team restructures, one of my staff said to me that 'the way we're being treated is disgusting and someone needs to pay' – but, again, I didn't take much notice. I just thought she was ranting and needed to get her frustrations off her chest. I probably would have taken more notice if I'd thought the person who going to 'pay' was me!

Now, I'm a big fan of change – I love variety and the opportunity to do things differently and better – but the change that took place in this team at the time was excessive, even for me. Following the restructure, we went through a 'business reshuffle', to align teams to like-for-like functions. At the same time, we were consolidating state functions into a central location. And if those two things weren't enough, we were also outsourcing some of our function to a third party provider and offshoring a large part of the team's function to a team in India – all at the same time!

My team grew from 13 direct reports to 36, with recruitment taking up a large part of my time. When I wasn't interviewing, I was in project meetings discussing the changes or pleading with my manager to do something about the enormity of what was happening. My leader was great; he felt my pain and had as many conversations as he could with his leaders to slow things down but was constantly met with responses such as, 'We just have to get it done' or 'We don't have the time to slow down' – and one manager even said, 'Sometimes you just have to let the train derail!' I can't imagine the pressure this put him under, because he cared for his people and was doing everything he could to help out. However, we were pretty much on our own. It became clear the change wasn't going to end well and we were at the epicentre, hopelessly trying to make it work.

For months, I was pushed to my limits. I'm an action-oriented person by default, so the more there was to do, the less notice I took of my people. I conducted one-on-one discussions as simply ticking off an item from my to-do list – they were rushed and focused on results, and on getting these results on track if they were below standard. One of my senior officers was what I referred to at the time as 'resistant to change', and argued about every decision being made. He begrudgingly accepted what needed to be done when he was with me, but undermined me to the team to the point where I couldn't trust him at all.

Toward the end of implementing all these changes, my manager decided to take his leadership team on a retreat. We'd all been pushed to our limits and he recognised some time away from the business to clear our heads and see things from a new perspective was in order. And he was right! Spending two days with my peers was fantastic; it allowed me to reflect on the changes and how I was doing in my role. I knew I'd neglected my people and that they also were in need of some relief. I returned to the office feeling refreshed and ready to make things happen – and for the first week I was back, I felt really positive.

Then, one afternoon, I was called into my manager's office and told that while we were away my senior officer, along with some of my team, had started a petition to have me removed from the business. The petition was signed by most people in my team and given to the union to take action on. The union then sent a formal complaint to human resources within my organisation, who commenced an investigation into the claims being made. For the next three months, while continuing to manage the changes, I and my team were interviewed, as were my peers, managers and many other people I worked with. Everything I had done since entering the team was put under a microscope. And this was all while my son was only just one year old.

Shame and anger

My manager told me not to worry, that I'd done nothing wrong and that my team were on a witch-hunt. So I tried to take it in my stride and not think about it too much – but under the surface I was struggling and the stress I was feeling was causing physical issues. I started to get sick (I never get sick), my hair was falling out, my skin was cracking and peeling for no particular reason, I developed toothaches and neck pain, sore throats and common colds – you name it, I was picking it up. I was distant from my family, particularly from my son who was really demanding and who never slept through the night (until he was about four years old). I didn't know about vulnerability at the time, so I kept most of my emotions hidden under the surface and carried on like everything was fine.

I'll never forget the day my manager called me into his office and delivered the outcome of the investigation – although what he actually said is a bit of a blur. All I heard was that the company was going to issue me with a written warning for bullying and intimidation – a first and final written warning. In other words, the worst warning you can get! They'd found that I'd breached a core code of conduct and were taking it very seriously. At that moment, everything slowed down. With the message that had been delivered, everything hit me like a fully loaded freight train, and there was no going back from that.

My manager still maintained that I'd been singled out and unfairly treated, and he refused to actually issue me with the warning. So for months I sat in limbo. While it was great that my manager believed in me and did all he could to protect me, the pressure of the 'train derailing' wore him down too. A few months later, he took a role in another part of the organisation and moved on. In the absence of having someone to protect me from the supposed 'witch-hunt', the written warning was soon issued by another manager. The letter was given to me and I was informed of the consequences of my actions if they continued in the future – that is, I would be removed from the organisation. I was put on a performance management plan to be rehabilitated and asked to formally apologise to my team in face-to-face meetings.

I have never, in my life, felt as broken as I did in that moment … I had hit rock bottom!

I remember the apology feeling a lot like a public shaming – like walking through the crowded streets naked for everyone to stare at and make fun of. I drafted the apology I would read from, and this was reviewed and adjusted by my new manager and HR. When it was deemed correct, I stood in front of my team and read it out. Leading up to the delivery of my apology, I felt sick to my stomach, I couldn't eat and I couldn't sleep. I had so many emotions flowing through me and I had no idea what to do with them all. So I tried to suppress the emotions and think about things logically. But all I was met with were questions – what exactly was I apologising for? I had never ever been given feedback that the way I treated my people was wrong. I had never been given feedback about my performance being anything less than great – in fact, in my numerous previous roles in the organisation, I had been rated as the highest performer year after year and had never failed to deliver what was expected of me. So what had happened? Who was I? Was I really a bully? Had I really got this whole leadership thing so completely wrong? Why hadn't someone told me I was a bully? Why had I worked so hard, sacrificed so many moments with my son, my husband and my friends to work late and get things done? Where were the loyalty and the appreciation for what I was doing for the business?

I had worked harder in that role than any other role in my professional life, and from a process perspective the changes were implemented successfully, but I had still failed

– and I never saw it coming. I had no idea that this could ever happen to me, and I was completely taken by surprise. I remember walking around my neighbourhood one weekend (I'd needed to get out of the house and walking was my thing at the time) when my older sister called to see how I was doing. I told her I'd given up, it was pointless trying to fight, I had no more energy and I had no-one to back me. I had failed and I thought the only way out was to quit. I had devoted six years to an organisation that, at that stage, I felt had betrayed me. I had sacrificed my health, my fitness and my relationship with my son and my husband – all to deliver results that in the end didn't matter.

I remember my sister yelling at me, 'Don't you dare give up, Shell. You've worked so hard to be where you are right now and if you quit it will all be for nothing.' She lectured me for about 4 kilometres and by the end I knew she was right. Everything she said was what I needed to hear. Now wasn't the time to quit, even though it would have definitely been the easiest thing to do. She helped me work out how I was going to read the apology to my team and how to resume my role as a leader of the team I'd so hopelessly failed … and I was going to have to dig deep.

Playing the victim

So, on the day I was to deliver my apology to the team, I treated it like a stage performance in a play. I got up there in front of my team and gave the performance of my life. I read that letter with every emotion and gesture needed to convincingly deliver my message – and none of it was real! It meant nothing to me. I didn't mean a single word that was written. How could I? I was so angry, hurt, betrayed and completely broken. I hated everyone. I saw other people getting away with behaviour that I'd been given a warning about and I seethed. Why had I been punished for something so many other managers did? Why wasn't I given an opportunity to improve like everyone else? My new manager wasn't an inspiration either; in fact, he exacerbated how I was feeling. He once called his leadership team into a room to ask us what was going on with the data, before telling us 'Data doesn't lie, people do!' How could he say that? How could he refer to his leaders as liars and still remain in his role? I definitely wasn't embracing vulnerability at this stage; instead, I was in serious victim mode and was hyper-critical of everything everyone around me was doing.

I'm not sure how long I played the victim. For months, I just went through the motions and, for the first time in my working life, I only did what was asked of me – no more, no less. I stopped managing my team and instead just approved leave and granted access when required. I conducted one-on-one conversations that ticked the box but didn't address poor performance or cover development opportunities. I just let them be. I moved from being a 'responsive leader' to a 'dysfunctional leader' where I was withdrawn (refer to chapter 4 for a refresher on these leader types). I only worked 40 hours a week and when I left for the day that was it. I stopped logging back in when my son went to bed. I spent quality time with my son and my husband and I pondered life, trying to work out where I would go from here. I couldn't stay in my current role but I was going to struggle to get another role. I had been 'red-flagged', which meant that for the next 12 months I had to disclose my warning to any potential hiring managers and I missed out on a pay increase and bonuses (first-world problems, I know, but remember I was a top performer so this hurt).

I went to leadership courses and did everything that was expected of me and eventually I got a role in another business as a senior business analyst. As it was a projects role I didn't have any direct reports, so I wasn't a risk to the business. This role was a great place to heal and consider what I wanted my professional life to be. It was in this role that I decided I wasn't going to remain in the corporate world and that more was out there. While I didn't know what it was at that point, I was suddenly open to possibility.

Realising I'm not super-human and embracing my vulnerability

Over the following seven years, I learnt about vulnerability along with so many other things relating to leadership and development and how people think. I really did go on a journey of self-discovery, one that I remain on today, to find a better version of myself. I came to acknowledge and accept my own role in the events that led to my written warning. I learnt how to lead, not command and control, to influence people around me and to bring out their best version of themselves. I became a leader who wasn't just focused on results at the expense of my people and a leader who wasn't just focused on people at the expense of my results. I found the happy balance between the two and I learnt to have conversations in a way that wasn't confronting or intimidating but delivered the required message. I learnt to lead without being a bully.

I'm so happy I'm not super-human and I'm grateful for the opportunities that being vulnerable has presented. If I can share the most vulnerable experience of my career and still be okay, what can you do to make the difference with your team and your career?

> *Great leaders don't try to be perfect. Great leaders try to be themselves. And that's what makes them great.*
>
> **Simon Sinek**

Trust

> **trust**
> *noun*
> 1. Firm belief in the reliability, truth, or ability of someone or something.

How each of us defines and establishes trust is different. For some people, trust is given upfront and as the relationship progresses the trust either diminishes or is maintained. For others, trust is something that must be earned and can only build gradually as a relationship evolves.

Regardless of how a person establishes trust, it is absolutely essential that trust be nurtured throughout a relationship. The most sustainable way for a leader to do this is to focus on everything we've been discussing in this chapter – that is, acting with authenticity, integrity and vulnerability! When you say what you mean, do what you say and are imperfectly human, you will deepen the trust you have with your staff. (Refer to figure 8.1 at the start of this chapter for how this is shown in the Dynamic Leadership model.)

Patrick Lencioni, author of *The Five Dysfunctions of a Team*, talks about trust being the foundation to highly cohesive teams. According to Lencioni:

> *Trust is the confidence among team members that their peers' intentions are good, and that there is no reason to be protective or careful around the group. Teammates are vulnerable with one another; they are confident that their respective vulnerabilities will not be used against them.*

Without a high level of trust, staff will withhold their opinion and avoid contributing to important discussions. They will tell you what they think you want to hear rather than what they believe to be true. Relationships will remain superficial without a high level of trust, and issues can manifest and become real problems over time.

As I've spoken about throughout this chapter, if you want your staff to have a deep level of trust with you and with each other, it's up to you to take the first step. You have to trust that you can speak honestly and openly with them and share your failures and lessons from past experiences. Only through demonstrating that you're serious about the relationship will your staff reciprocate.

Trusting other perspectives and values

The other thing to be aware of, as a leader, is your natural gravitation to those who are most like you. I remember in my early days as a leader walking into a room of people and gravitating to those who were like me, and avoiding those who were not like me. I was able to build trust with people who saw the world in a similar way to me but my trust eroded with those who saw it differently. I held on to my view of the world so tightly that I wasn't willing to see things from their perspective, nor was I taking the time to understand them. It was obvious that I treated people differently in the team, which then created an unstable and fractured culture of 'us' and 'them'.

When you feel like you don't trust someone, rather than creating distance between yourself and them, move closer. This seems counter-intuitive and feels super awkward but it brings great success. You see, it's really hard not to connect and build trust with people as you learn more about who they are, where they've come from and how they view the world.

Take the time to understand what's important to them, what their values are and how they might be different to your own values.

Values are what we deem to be the most important things in our lives. They are the basis for the decisions we make, how we differentiate between right and wrong and determine our behaviour. Our values are very much our compass in life – they guide us to make the right decision and prevent us from doing the wrong thing. The interesting thing about values is they're not generally at the front of our minds, but instead sit in the background and 'passively' influence everything that's going on.

However, other people's values can become obvious if you take notice and observe how people react and respond to different situations and use different words. When investing in relationships, you will start to notice the role values play and the influence they have over levels of trust. Take the time to understand the values of your staff, once you've developed a good level of trust and your staff feel comfortable opening up about their values.

The one thing that will erode trust faster than anything else is compromising someone's values. If someone has a high value around respect and they attach 'being on time' to 'having respect', being late will automatically compromise the value and erode trust. If you are late continually, you will damage the relationship. Similarly, if someone has a high value around family and 'attending their children's events' is how they fulfil their 'family' value, getting in the way of that happening will also compromise the value and have an impact on relationships.

So even when you think something isn't important, because it's not aligned to your own values, this doesn't mean it's not important to your staff.

Drilling deeper when understanding values

Along with recognising and trusting perspectives and values different to your own, you can use the following steps to delve deeper into your staff's values and understand them in the context of work. These steps have been adapted by Mei Ouw from the process outlined in *Time Line Therapy*, by Tad James and Wyatt Woodsmall.

To better understand your staff's values at work, try the following:

1. Set aside an hour to meet with each staff member, or incorporate this discussion into their monthly one-on-one discussion.
2. Find a quiet room where you won't be distracted and bring a piece of paper and a pen.
3. Talk to your staff member about what values are and seek their permission to run a values exercise, explaining the context and purpose for doing so.
4. Ask your staff member what's important to them in the context of their career.
5. Write a list of all their responses, exactly how they say them. For example, they might reply, 'To feel heard' or 'Excitement'.
6. When your staff member has exhausted all the things that are important to them, ask them again what is important to them in the context of their career.

7. Allow them the silence to consider more possibilities and continue writing anything additional on the list.
8. Ask a third time, 'What's important to you in the context of your career?' and wait to see if anything else comes up.
9. Then ask them, 'Of all these things on the list, what's the one thing that would make you leave if you didn't have it?' Write down their response.
10. Then ask, 'Okay, so even if you weren't getting [the thing that would cause them to leave], what would make you stay?' Write down their response.

You now have a complete list of the things that are important to your staff member in the context of their career, so it's time to put them in order. Here's how:

1. Give the piece of paper to your staff member and ask them to number all their values in order of importance (with #1 given to the most important, #2 to the next important and so on) until all the values have a number beside them.
2. Rewrite their top six values (these are the most significant) in order and then ask your staff member to indicate whether they're currently being met with a 'Y' for yes or 'N' for no.
3. Ask, 'For the values that are not currently being met, what could you change or what action could you take to meet this value?' Get them to write down the actions.
4. Finally, ask, 'What support do you need from me to ensure you're aligning to your values?' and agree on any changes you need to make as their leader.

If your staff's values do not align with the organisation's values, a conversation like this might be enough for them to realise this isn't the right place for them to be and they need to explore other organisations that might better align. It might also be a great opportunity to identify where an individual's values do align and reconnect them with the organisation.

What about loyalty?

I want to go off on a slight tangent and talk about loyalty for a moment. Loyalty is a popular value that surfaces when talking to staff about what's important and I think it is an interesting value in today's workplace. In the past, loyalty was built on tenure and how long a person remained with an organisation or in a role.

Now, with the pace of change, and the demand from consumers to do faster, better, cheaper or different, it's hard to retain staff purely based on the time they've been with the business. Staff retention and promotion now needs to be based on what the business needs and what will result in success and future survival.

In many large corporate organisations, restructures take place annually and, as a result, roles are made redundant. This means good people are sometimes let go. So the meaning staff place on loyalty needs to change. An organisation that carries unnecessary roles because they like the person in the role or because that person has been there for so long isn't making good business decisions – and, financially, this hurts.

Redundancies and restructures don't mean the organisation or leader doesn't value loyalty; they just mean they see loyalty as a different priority or playing a different role in today's environment.

When I'm speaking with people who do value loyalty, I will often ask how they would define it and then start to challenge their thinking around the definition and how it would realistically play out in a successful organisation.

If someone has been with the organisation for a long time and their performance has deteriorated to mediocre, should I keep them purely because of the time they've been with the business? Probably not. And I would ask, 'Who's responsible for that drop in performance?' Often loyalty is a convenient excuse for staff to coast and not try as hard over time.

But, if they're constantly evolving, learning new skills and adapting to new challenges, they could easily fit into future roles as the organisation changes. It is then that loyalty will play an important role. If two people are achieving the same exciting things but one has been with the organisation longer, most of the time the one with the longer history will be the one to stay. In this scenario, loyalty is the deciding factor. But most of the time staff aren't privy to this information and, therefore, don't see it playing out.

If you expect an organisation to be loyal to you, you must also demonstrate that you are willing to do what it takes to adapt over time. That means improving your performance year on year and avoiding becoming too comfortable in your role.

Remember, superficial conversations and superficial acts of kindness will lead to superficial levels of trust. Your team will play nice, for a while, but they won't perform at their peak and often won't deliver results consistently.

When you understand what is important to your people, it becomes easier to adjust your language, how you communicate with them and how you behave so as to continue to build trust over time. It's all about moving closer, and we explore this more in the next chapter.

For now, keep in mind that we trust what we know, so get to know your staff – all of your staff – more and the trust will grow, as will your relationships!

CHAPTER 9
INSPIRE RESPECT

I have a theory that you can't respect someone you don't like. Sure, you can respect a decision that someone has made without liking that person but I don't see how you can respect the person. While this is my theory right now, I am open to different ways of seeing things. So if you fundamentally disagree I'd love to have a chat with you.

If we go with this, however – that to respect someone, you must like them – then investing in relationships becomes your first priority. If your staff know you, trust you and feel like they can be themselves around you, creating an environment for them to respect you shouldn't be too complicated.

As a leader, you want your staff to respect not only you but also their colleagues, business partners, stakeholders, and the wider network that they operate within. This, for some teams, might also include respecting your customers. So what does it mean to respect someone else?

In this chapter, I cover why respect is a fundamental part of building a dynamic team, and outline how to inspire your people to respect you and see that they have a role just as important as you to be true to themselves and those around them.

Figure 9.1 shows how inspiring respect in your staff is the second core component of the Dynamic Leadership model, and one that leads to strong engagement.

Figure 9.1: The Dynamic Leadership model and the say, do, be of respect

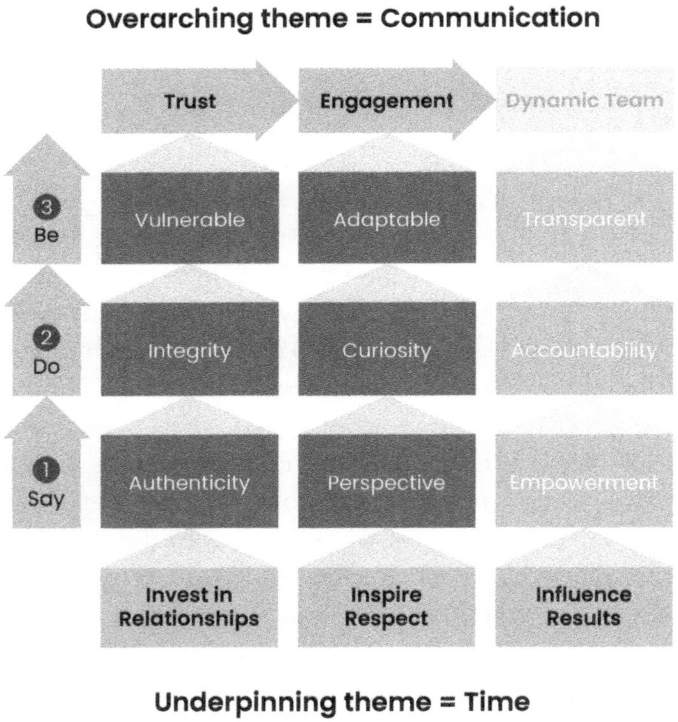

As shown in figure 9.1, respect is first about seeing other perspectives and acknowledging that no-one is ever right and no-one is ever wrong. There are no 'right' ways to do things and no 'wrong' ways to do things, just different ways. When we can learn to take on different perspectives, we can learn to respect different points of view.

Next, respect is about showing curiosity and exploring the gap we need to close to reach our full potential as leaders. This requires patience and an openness to listen. Finding a leader who truly listens – not a leader who simply hears what they think they need to and responds – is very rare. In this chapter, we discuss how leaders who listen also become really good at asking questions that evoke understanding and remove judgement.

Finally, respect is about being adaptable and using your full spectrum of communication skills to determine the optimal approach, depending on the context and audience for a given situation.

It is when we are willing to take on a different perspective and have the curiosity to listen and ask questions (without applying judgement) and then adapt our style to suit the context and the audience that we inspire our staff to respect us – and increase engagement.

Respect or fear?

In the past, respect was demanded; leaders operated from a position of power and control, and staff responded out of fear. Today respect is earned and leaders must operate from a position of influence, which means creating deep, meaningful relationships and being able to encourage creative thinking and challenge differing views. Today's leaders must do what it takes to get the best out of their people and deliver the best for the business.

Similar to many other aspects of leadership covered in this book, inspiring others starts with you and how inspired you feel about yourself, your role and your potential. It relates to your ability to build confidence around what you know and what you're capable of achieving through your people. And this confidence is built on humility and not propped up by ego.

In *The Multiplier Effect*, authors Liz Wiseman, Lois Allen and Elise Foster talk about two kinds of leaders:

1. *The Diminisher:* The leader who 'drains intelligence, energy, and capability from the people around them and needs to be the smartest person in the room'. These types of leaders are the 'idea killers, the energy sappers, the diminishers of talent and capability'.
2. *The Multiplier:* The leader at the other end of the spectrum. These leaders 'use their intelligence to amplify the smarts and capabilities of the people around them. When these leaders walk into a room, light bulbs go on; ideas flow and problems get solved. These leaders use their smarts to make everyone around them smarter and more capable'.

I think respect is generated when a leader is a 'multiplier' and I think respect is lost when leaders are 'diminishers' or start to take over. So if you are a leader who builds or maintains your confidence through ego and consumes the spotlight, you have a lot of work to do. You might have the attention of your staff but you definitely won't have their respect.

So start with working on the respect you have for yourself and then turn your attention to your team, starting with their different perspectives.

Perspective

> **perspective**
> *noun*
> 1. A particular attitude towards or way of regarding something; a point of view.

How we form our perspectives comes from past experiences and how we make sense of incoming information based on our filters to 'delete', 'distort' and 'generalise'.

According to the neurolinguistic programming (NLP) model of communication, we have around 2 million bits of information per second available to us at any given time. This information is presented through our six senses: auditory (what we hear), visual (what we see), kinaesthetic (what we feel), auditory digital (what we say to ourselves), olfactory (what we smell), and gustatory (what we taste).

Of all this information, we are only able to absorb around 134 bits per second, meaning that a lot of information presented to us is simply not taken in (see figure 9.2).

How we determine what information we take in and what information we ignore will depend on what we believe to be relevant at any given point. And what we deem to be relevant will depend on past experiences and how we make sense of the world – in other words, we run filters.

The filters we use:

- 'delete' information we don't see as relevant at the time
- 'distort' information that we may not completely understand and make it mean something it's perhaps not
- 'generalise' information by assessing it and putting it into a category that is easy to understand.

Figure 9.2: Average capacity to take in 134 bits of information per second

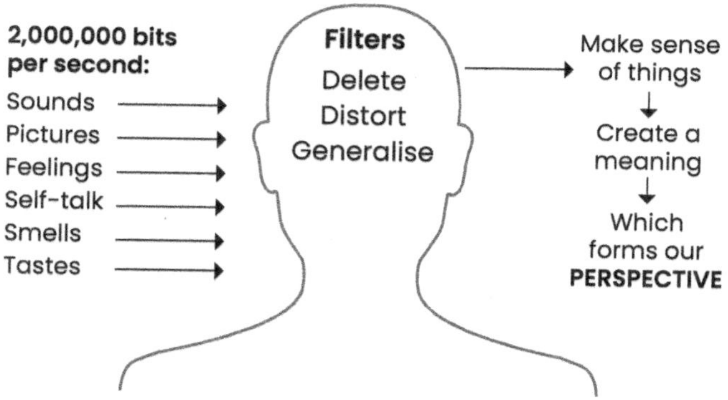

To clarify this a little more, here's an example of how each filter might be applied for a person:

- *Delete:* When attending a meeting to learn more about a new product or service, you may not notice the patterns on the carpet or the slight whir of the air-conditioning. You are focused on the host and what they're saying about the product or service, and everything around that is deleted.
- *Distort:* When you're driving your car into a parking space, you put your foot on the brake at exactly the same time as the car beside you starts to move. This creates a feeling that you're still moving – like an illusion. Another example of a distortion is when you bump into someone in a department store, turn quickly to apologise … and see you're talking to a mannequin!
- *Generalise:* When you see an L-shaped frame with four legs at the base, you likely assume it's a chair. Or when

you see a person dressed in a suit, you might assume they are important, or that a person in a high-visibility vest is a tradesperson.

The filters we use allow us to be efficient, to make decisions quickly and effectively get things done. The filters we use and how we make sense of the information creates our perspective – which isn't necessarily true or false and isn't necessarily right or wrong. It's just different. Our perspective isn't everyone's reality, just our own. (Byron Lewis's *Magic of NLP Demystified* outlines these concepts in much more detail – see Sources at the end of this book.)

Getting into your staff's heads

The following table shows some examples of these different perspectives playing out in the workplace, comparing your staff's behaviour and thinking with your thinking.

Their behaviour	Your thinking	Their thinking
Avoiding eye contact	*They're hiding something and can't be trusted.*	*I'm feeling so intimidated right now, I wish the world would open up and swallow me whole.*
Disagreeing with an opinion	*They're a wet blanket and just want to shoot down everyone's ideas.*	*I'm really concerned about the risk this solution exposes us to and want to make sure we don't set ourselves up for failure.*

Their behaviour	Your thinking	Their thinking
Saying 'yes' but doing the opposite	*They're just paying me lip service; they don't even care.*	*I accept your point of view but I disagree and I don't want to cause any conflict so I'll just nod.*
Screwing their face up when feedback is given	*They don't respect me or care about the role I play.*	*Wow! Your breath is really ripe this morning. Maybe ease off on the coffee and cigarettes a little, I'm feeling nauseous.*
Talking about you in a negative way when you're not around	*They're superficial and they backstab.*	*I really don't agree with the way you manage the team but there's no way I'm having that conversation with you.*
Falling asleep in meetings	*They don't care about the organisation; it's just a job to them.*	*I've been up all night with sick children, the temperature in this room is too warm and I'm not sure what you're talking about.*
Taking sick leave on a regular basis	*They're trying to piss me off; it's just a game to them.*	*'I feel really unmotivated and getting out of bed is a massive struggle so I prefer to call in sick than face a day in a place that makes me terribly unhappy.*

Their behaviour	Your thinking	Their thinking
Frowning when you attempt to make conversation	*They think they're better than me.*	*Okay, this better be good; it's taken me an hour to get in the right frame of mind to complete this task so I don't want to let it go too quickly.*

So, how do you know what your staff are thinking? Well, unless you outright ask them, you won't. I'm not saying don't assume, because making assumptions is a necessary part of our lives. What I'm saying is be open to other possibilities and go with the assumption that your staff are well intended and, whatever their behaviour, it comes from a good place!

This can be hard to get your head around when so many of us agree on the common meaning behind things such as cars, doors and fridges. It is easy to assume that because we both agree that a door is a door, we must also agree that someone who's loud is obnoxious – when actually we might think quite differently.

When you are open to different perspectives, you learn to let go of the tight grip you have on your reality and start to appreciate the variety of different realities that exist. And when you do this, anything is possible. You can see that your options are endless and that rather than changing the people around you, you can simply change the meaning you've given something.

Changing your thinking

So how do you change your perspective? Well, you can start to notice how other people view the same situation as you and consider seeing things from their point of view. Or, you can ask yourself these questions about a specific event that has generated a high level of emotion:

- *What happened?* Jot down what actually took place, not what you made it mean. For example, a tall man dressed in a navy blue suit walked into the room, looked around the room and then sat in an empty chair.
- *What did you make it mean?* Write down the meaning you gave to what took place. For example, an arrogant senior manager walked into the room, saw me, a young nervous woman sitting to one side of the room, and decided he didn't want to be seen near me because I might make him look bad or ruin his image so he sat in the furthest chair away. He definitely doesn't like me.
- *What else could it mean?* Write down all the other possible meanings for the situation. For example, the man sat in the chair closest to the door so as not to interrupt the meeting that had already commenced. The man might be recovering from an ear infection and still struggling to hear so he found a chair closest to the speaker. The man sat in the first empty chair he saw so as not to draw too much attention to himself. And so on.
- *Why are you choosing to make it mean ...?* Consider the purpose behind the original meaning you gave the event. Write down what advantages and disadvantages you gain from making it mean that thing. For example, I have a high need to be liked so when I think someone doesn't

like me, I think the worst of them to make myself feel better. It is my protection strategy.

- *What would be the benefit of shifting your perspective?* Consider the benefits of taking on a different perspective.

If you were to practise these questions every time you felt frustrated, upset or annoyed at a situation, you'd be likely to quickly loosen your grip on your own perspective and start to look at things differently. You would start to see the gaps in your current way of thinking and look for alternatives. You would realise that a lot of the perspectives you (and all of us) have are for self-preservation and don't encourage constant learning and growth.

Taking on different perspectives is about forming new habits through repetition and challenging yourself to think differently about things. Even if it feels uncomfortable, keep going because the outcome will be more positive than any initial thinking you may have had.

Changing what you focus on

I love the TED Talk 'Perspective is everything' by Rory Sutherland, which is centred on the value of changing what we focus on. One example he uses in this talk is that £6 million was spent on reducing the train journey between Paris and London by 40 minutes. Sutherland argues for 0.01 per cent of this cost, they could have installed wi-fi to improve the enjoyment and usefulness of the journey. And for around 10 per cent of cost, you could have top models handing out Château Pétrus to all the passengers and 'people would ask for the trains to be slowed down!'

By changing how we view a situation, we can change the way we feel about it.

Changing your perspective

I'll end this section with a little experience I had with my sons that helped me to see things from their point of view.

I had had a long day at work, and my daughter was still quite young and was very demanding of my attention. The only time I got to myself was after the kids went to bed. This particular night, the boys were continually getting up out of bed to ask me questions or tell me things:

- 'Can I get a drink of water?'
- 'Can you sign my permission form?'
- 'I have to go to the toilet.'
- 'I need a cuddle.'
- 'I love you mum.'

And so on and so on … I eventually got frustrated with the constant interruptions to whatever I was watching on Netflix at the time and yelled, 'GO TO BED, SHUT THE DOOR, GO TO SLEEP AND DON'T COME OUT AGAIN!' The boys quickly ran into their room and closed the door. There was silence and peace and I continued watching my show.

About 10 minutes later, I noticed a piece of paper slip out from under the door of the boys' bedroom. I smiled, paused Netflix again and retrieved the piece of paper, which turned out to be a handwritten note. The note said (with minor errors corrected):

> *If you're tired just go to bed and we're sorry for being so difficult.* ☹ *XOXO Love Luis and Riley.*

I love that they saw my outburst as a result of being tired – and I actually had to consider whether it was caused by tiredness. I also like their simple solution for tiredness – just go to bed – and then pondered how often I used the same line with them. It was a great opportunity to see how they have formed their perspective.

My boys are a great mirror for how I behave, how others perceive my behaviour and how I form my own perspectives. If you don't have a mirror, someone who can challenge your thinking and perspective, perhaps now would be a great time to go find one!

Curiosity

curiosity
noun
1. A strong desire to know or learn something.
2. An unusual or interesting object or fact.

Once a leader becomes open to taking on different perspectives, curiosity comes easier. For a leader to be truly curious, they must set their judgement aside and assume an openness to learning, even when they think they know all they need to. They recognise that their point of view isn't the only point of view and are not overly critical of those who don't share a similar way of thinking. They appreciate that there's more than one way to peel a banana.

Distraction note: Did you know that monkeys peel their bananas starting from the opposite end to what most humans do? They use the stem as a handle, which apparently makes the banana easier to hold, plus opening from the other end means you don't need to remove the stringy bits!

How we peel a banana isn't right or wrong, it's just different. So, let's not judge different; let's just be more curious.

To become more curious as a leader, you should focus on three things: how you listen, how you ask and the power of the pause. Let's take a look at all three.

How you listen

First, there is a lot more to 'listening' than what we will cover in this chapter! I am sharing only one of many different perspectives that exist. So read on with the intention of being curious, not judgemental!

When a leader develops a strong desire to learn about someone or something, they are more likely to listen with greater attention. When we're in the middle of a complex task, however, and a staff member interrupts us, we may not be so eager to give our full attention and listen with curiosity.

So the first rule of becoming a curious listener is to create an optimal time and appropriate environment to have the conversations. Don't expect to be able to switch from doing a task that requires deep focus straight into listening with curiosity the minute you're interrupted. Minimise as many of these interruptions as possible and start to put aside time for the conversations towards the end of the day (when you've completed your important tasks). Setting specific times might mean when a staff member interrupts you that you ask if you could meet later in the day when you have a little more time. Often I see leaders who encourage staff to come to them whenever they have a question and so enable behaviour that isn't sustainable. This often means the staff don't need to think for themselves because you've essentially offered to do it for them. If they need urgent support, you would make exceptions but you'll find most interruptions are out of habit more than a true need.

When it's time to have the conversation, consider moving to an environment where there are minimal distractions. Depending on the topic being discussed, the best space might be a meeting room, coffee shop or going outside to walk in the park. Make sure your phone is on silent too so it's not a distraction.

The next rule to becoming a curious listener is to listen with a 'we' focus rather than a 'me' focus. When you're listening with a 'me' focus, you're really not invested in the conversation; instead, you're only making a token attempt and this doesn't go unnoticed. As shown in figure 9.3, when listening with a 'me' focus, only three levels of listening are possible.

Figure 9.3: Levels of listening

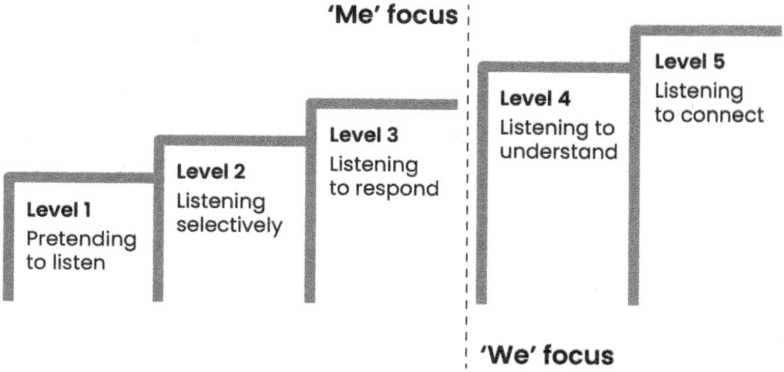

At level one you are *pretending to listen*. You may nod and feign interest at intervals throughout a conversation while you're actually distracted thinking about or doing something else. This usually happens when someone interrupts you at your desk and you don't ask to make time later – so you continue the task you're doing and try or pretend to listen to the staff member. This is overtly obvious to the person you're talking to and unless they already know the answer or are just looking for a 'yes' from you, the conversation is generally pointless.

At level two you are *selectively listening*. This is where your attention is divided between the conversation and something else. You are listening for keywords to respond to and absorb only a fraction of the information being provided. It is common for leaders who like only high-level snapshots or headline pieces of information to do this when they're speaking with someone who speaks in a lot of detail and gives a lot of information. You may zone out while the person is sharing information that you don't deem to be valuable, and then zone back in when you hear certain keywords. Listening in this way doesn't open up curiosity and often you miss the opportunity to learn about how the other person thinks and the context surrounding what is being said.

At level three you are *listening to respond*. I've found this is where most leaders sit. You hear just enough to get the general idea of the conversation and then start thinking through your response. Once you've come up with the response you may interrupt, try to finish their sentence or 'pretend to listen' until they've finished and immediately share your response. Similar to selectively listening, when listening to respond you can misunderstand where the other person is coming from and how their point of view has been formed.

The 'me' focus stages of listening are generally ineffective and a big waste of time for both parties – and, they erode trust. For a leader to become good at listening they need to operate from a 'we' focus position, which opens up two further levels of listening.

At level four you are *listening to understand*. This is where you become fully present with the person you're speaking to. You give your full attention, clear your mind and remove all distractions, along with the need to get the conversation over quickly. When you listen to understand, you will be curious about the content and the context. You often will not respond immediately to what the other person is saying. You will wait until the other person has finished speaking before considering your own response. This means the conversation will have gaps of silence throughout. So, if you're someone who doesn't like silence, you may feel quite awkward or uncomfortable to begin with, but stick with it because the feeling will soon pass. It is the silence that allows what has been said to be fully absorbed and allows you to consider a number of possible responses and uncover the one which would be most appropriate for the situation.

At level five you are *listening to connect*. This is where you set judgement aside, clear your mind of any assumptions and fully listen. You are listening not only for content and context, but also for the other person's thought processes and how they came to certain conclusions. You will listen to appreciate their perspective, even when it differs from your own, and become aware of how they use their delete-distort-generalise filters to get to the point they're at. You will find that the more you listen to connect, the more you will build a deeper level of trust and the more the other person will respect you. It's also where the other person will learn to listen in a similar way. It's through listening to connect that it's hard to dislike someone, because the more you know about someone, the more you respect their views and ways of thinking.

When you listen with a 'we' focus, you allow your staff to feel heard, feel like their opinion matters and feel like they're contributing to something bigger than themselves. Not enough people in the world listen but we all want to feel heard. It's a dilemma that can be solved by each individual learning 'how' to listen to connect – that's where you'll inspire respect!

How you ask

To demonstrate true curiosity, listening will only get you halfway. The other half comes from your ability to ask questions. And it's not just any questions but powerful questions that evoke further thought or challenge ways of thinking.

So let's take a look at some powerful questions that you could consider asking your staff in your next conversation with them.

Contrary to popular belief, asking 'why' isn't always the best question, but is really powerful when trying to understand the intrinsic motivators driving a person's actions. I use the 'why' question to understand what's important to my clients, to help them gain clarity in their direction and set a vision and goals for the future.

Where I wouldn't ask 'why?' is when I want staff to consider other alternatives to a situation.

One of my clients, the owner of a fast-growing business, was feeling frustrated with his staff being late to work each morning. He couldn't understand why their behaviour continued, despite repeated conversations about getting to work on time. When I asked him to talk me through the conversation he said he would simply ask his staff, 'Why were you late?'

His staff would respond quickly with myriad reasons, such as 'traffic was terrible', 'my wife forgot to set the alarm' or 'I couldn't get the kids in the car'. All valid reasons and all focused on the staff member justifying and reinforcing their behaviour. In this type of conversation, asking 'why' actually prevented the staff member from seeing things from a different perspective and considering the impact of their actions on the people around them and the performance of the business.

To get his staff to take responsibility for their punctuality, my client had to change the way he was asking his questions. Instead of asking, 'Why were you late?' he started to ask the following questions to open up the conversation and get his staff to come to their own conclusion on the impacts of their tardiness:

- 'I notice you were late this morning. *What* happened?'
- '*What* might be the impact of you being late?' (And then continue to ask 'What else?' until the staff member has exhausted the list of potential impacts.)
- '*How* might you do things differently to ensure you get to work on time?' (Again, ask 'What else?' until they have exhausted the list of potential impacts.)
- '*When* will you commit to making this change?'
- '*Where* will you make this change?'
- '*Who* might be able to support you through this change?'

And the final question is this: 'Do you need any support from me?'

The power of the pause

The final component to becoming curious – let's call this the cherry on top – is your ability to hold the silence. I call this the 'power of the pause'.

It is only through the 'pause' that our brains switch on and we can think more deeply about things.

Research conducted by Mary Rowe in schools in 1974 (and outlined in Sondra Napell's 'Six Common Non-Facilitating Teaching Behaviors' – see Sources) found that students, when asked a question, needed 'more than just a few seconds to process information and formulate a response'. When this doesn't occur, students were more likely to grow a dependence upon the teacher to do their thinking for them. Rowe argued that when the teacher becomes a non-stop talker, students have no chance to think over what is being said, to formulate intelligent responses, or to ask for clarification.

When you apply this to your team, you may see why staff are reluctant to 'speak up' or think for themselves. I have observed many monthly one-on-one discussions where the leader doesn't wait any longer than one to two seconds before offering a solution, rephrasing or providing hints on the answer. If the staff member remains quiet long enough, the conversation will simply carry on … and so will any undesired behaviour!

This dependence can also extend to staff wanting confirmation on the smallest decisions, making it very difficult for the team to continue to perform in the absence of their leader.

To break behaviours of dependence, and to bring out the best in your ability to listen and ask, create a habit of 'pausing' after you ask a question. Try counting to five slowly in your head – one-one thousand, two-one thousand, three-one thousand, four-one thousand, five-one thousand … for as long as it takes for your staff member to respond.

Rowe's research reported that when 'pause' time increased to three to five seconds:

- appropriate responses from students increased
- failure to respond decreased
- comparing data between themselves increased.

It is through a leader's curiosity that powerful questions can be formed, and this in turn encourages deeper thinking and a confidence from everyone to make better decisions.

Adaptable

adaptable
adjective
1. Able to adjust to new conditions.
2. Able to be modified for a new use or purpose.

What got you to where you are today won't be enough to get you to where you want to be tomorrow! One of the common mistakes new leaders make is assuming they can continue to work in the way they always have and continue to be successful. It's like the business that's still doing all their advertising through print newspapers and refusing to go online because that's what made them successful in the past! It's only a matter of time before they're no longer seen and have to close their doors.

Real-life example

Let me share with you a story about Brendan, who was an extremely talented individual. He was the highest performer in his team and was promoted into a leadership role after just eight months. When Brendan first stepped into the role, he led by example. He did his own work but also continued to pick up the slack from the rest of the team ... after all, his role now was to make the whole team successful. If the team saw him working hard, surely they would work harder.

After doing this solidly for six months, Brendan become unwell and was off work for two weeks. He knew the stresses of his role played a big part in his illness, and also knew something had to change. So he decided enough was enough and changed his leadership style to a position of authority – he became 'the boss'.

Over the next six months, Brendan gave orders, he alienated his team and slowly eroded the once vibrant team culture. Absenteeism increased and so did staff turnover. Brendan was at a loss – what was he doing wrong?!

So, here's the thing: no one-size-fits-all approach works with leadership. There isn't even an approach that would work for a whole day on its own. To be a successful leader and build a dynamic team, you must be adapting all of the time – to different people, to different situations, and in different contexts. And to adapt easily and effortlessly takes practice.

Using the six styles of leadership

To start working on adaptability, I encourage leaders to become familiar with Daniel Goleman's six styles of leadership (outlined in *Leadership That Gets Results* – see Sources at the back of this book). The six styles are simple to understand and you can easily identify which ones you do well and which ones you don't. You can then work on becoming good at all the styles so that when you need to adapt, each option will be natural and automatic.

The six styles are:

1. *Visionary/authoritative:* This style is intended to inspire and mobilise people toward a vision or future goal, with the leader taking a 'come with me' approach. This style works best when changes require new vision, or when a clear direction is needed.

2. *Affiliative:* This style is intended to create harmony and build emotional bonds, with a 'people come first' stance. It works best to heal rifts in a team or to motivate people during stressful circumstances.
3. *Democratic:* This style is intended to forge consensus through participation and using a 'what do you think?' approach. This style works best when building buy-in or consensus, or hoping to get input from valuable employees. When using this style, the leader must take the time to understand the views of all their staff – so definitely not the style to use when looking for a quick fix. If you have invested time in building relationships with your team, you're likely to understand what's important to them and what they would want. You may only need to bring your team together when the change is contentious or when you have a new person join. Other than that, the team are likely to trust that you have their interests front of mind.
4. *Coaching:* This style is intended to develop people for the future, using a 'try this' attitude. It works best when helping an employee improve performance or develop long-term strengths. If you were to have a default style that you'd use most of the time, this would be my preference. It encourages self-discovery and empowers staff to come up with their own solutions and course of action. It is the coaching style that will support you in building capability across your team.
5. *Commanding/coercive:* This style is intended to demand immediate compliance, with a 'do what I tell you!' stance. It works best in emergencies or during crisis situations where you need your team to move fast and without

question. You would use this style sparingly because the overall impact on the team is negative. Some staff may respond well to the directness and urgency of this style but most will be intimidated and hurt, so be careful about when to apply it.

6. *Pacesetting:* This style is intended to set high standards for performance, with the leader asking their staff to 'do as I do'. It works best when doubt exists among staff around the reality of achieving a certain thing or the task has never been done before. The leader working towards it shows that it is possible. This is the style where many leaders continue to 'do the work' and again is overly negative because of the high chance your team will continue to rely on you to pick up the slack when things get busy.

I say to the leaders that come to my training that 'commanding' and 'pacesetting' styles should be used like condiments, instead of the meal itself. Just a little of each will produce flavour and enhance the meal. Too much will ruin it completely!

Goleman's *Leadership That Gets Results* expands on each of the styles and gives some great ideas on how to adapt so grabbing a copy for reference or simply finding his model online and becoming familiar with it is a good idea.

Looking at intentions versus actions

Being adaptable means you never give up. You're always in search of different ways of doing things and motivating your staff. It bothers me when leaders say things such as the following:

- 'I've tried everything; it just doesn't work.' (When they've tried three things.)

- 'They're not cut out for the role.' (When they've left them to figure it out on their own.)
- 'They have a poor attitude.' (Because the leader hasn't worked on the relationship.)
- 'They should know how to do their job.' (But the leader hasn't invested time in teaching them.)
- 'They're resistant to change.' (When the leader has rushed something through and surprised everyone with it.)
- 'They take advantage of my kindness.' (When the leader says yes to everything and never challenges their staff.)

For every comment you make about why things won't work, there's a reason that points straight back to you and how you've led your staff to that point. Whenever the outcome is different from what you intended, that's feedback on your ability to read a situation and apply a certain approach. It is your feedback to try something different, and to continue to adapt until you get the right outcome.

I was introduced to a really simple model a few years ago (see figure 9.4) that helps to break this down. The model looks at three things: your intention, the action you took and the impact of that action.

What we tend to do is assume our intention was rejected rather than looking at the action we took to deliver it. The following provides an example.

Figure 9.4: The intention, action, impact model

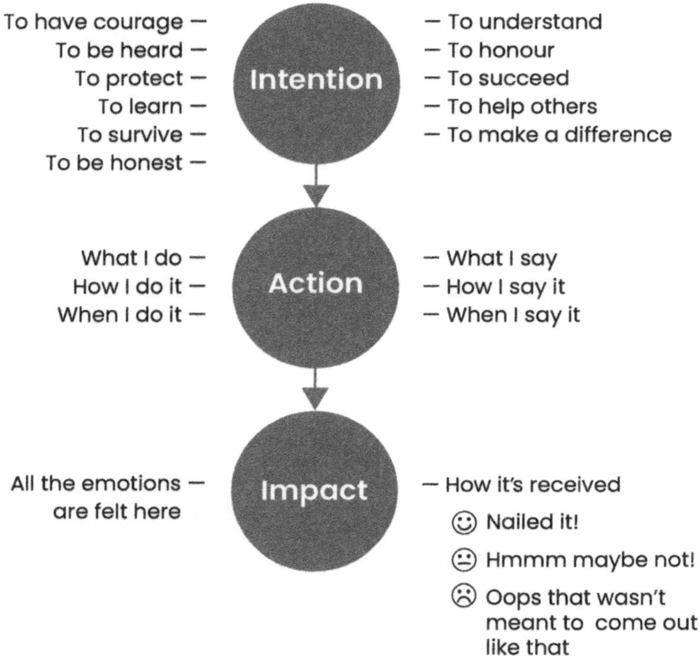

Real-life example

Sandra noticed that every time her staff member Robyn answered the phone she was abrupt and monotone, yet when speaking with someone face to face she had melody in her voice and was really warm. Sandra wanted Robyn to become aware of her change in behaviour. The following breaks down what Sandra did into her intention, action and impact:

- *Sandra's intention*: To help Robyn build awareness and build better relationships with people over the phone. So her intent was positive.

- *Sandra's action*: Sandra plucked up the courage to give the feedback (which she usually avoided) and walked over to Robyn's desk, straight after Robyn had hung up the phone. She burst out with, 'Do you know you're a real cow when you speak to people on the phone? Ha ha ... You should change that!' This action was direct, forceful and used poor humour, catching Robyn by surprise.
- *Impact*: Robyn replied, 'Okay' and then took the rest of the week off as sick leave because she was so angry at Sandra for speaking to her like that, asking herself, 'Who does she think she is telling me I'm a cow? She's the real cow!' So, definitely a negative impact.

At this point, Sandra could easily conclude that Robyn didn't respond well to 'any feedback', making her not 'the right fit for the team'. She might start to distance herself even further from Robyn. Or she could look at the role she played in delivering a well-intended message and consider what she might do differently.

Here's how changing her action could lead to a different impact:

- *Sandra's action*: She made some objective notes of what she'd observed in the phone call Robyn had just taken. She then went to Robyn's desk and asked if she had a few minutes to have a chat. She found a meeting room that was casual and didn't have a table. She first asked Robyn if everything was okay. Then she framed the conversation with, 'I know you're working really hard on communication this year and that's a key area of focus so I'm wondering if you would be okay if I offered some feedback?' Sandra waited for Robyn to agree and then proceeded to share what she saw, heard, thought and felt. She then asked Robyn what she thought about the call upon reflection. The 'coaching' conversation continued with questions and offers of support. This action was still direct, but more considered and objective, and allowed Robyn the time to reflect and ask questions.

- *The impact*: Robyn is grateful that Sandra invested the time in her development and helped her to realise that her phone manner was having a negative impact on the way she might be perceived by people she spoke to over the phone. She also now knew what she could do to improve. Overall, it was a positive impact!

If you can focus on aligning your intention with the overall impact through the actions that YOU take, you'll start to see different outcomes. As the saying goes, 'If at first you don't succeed, try, try, try again' until you get it right. That's what being adaptable is all about.

I'll finish this section with a quote often attributed to Benjamin Franklin that relates well to adaptability:

> *Remember not only to say the right thing in the right place, but far more difficult still, to leave unsaid the wrong thing at the tempting moment.*

Engagement

Once you're open to different perspectives, committed to asking questions, curious to learn and adapting your approach for optimal outcomes, your staff will engage. They will commit, and they will 'buy in' to your vision, your direction for the future, your goals and, most importantly, to each other. They will be inspired by you to be like you. You will be the leader they will want to follow!

For staff to 'buy in' to a particular change, idea, vision or business approach, they need to feel like they 'get it'. They need to feel like they have been included as part of the solution.

Many leaders treat 'buy-in' like it's a simple conversation with their staff, which can be held just before the change is scheduled. They will bring everyone together in a room where they will tell them what's about to happen – kind of like your neighbour telling you they're having a massive party at their house on Saturday night so there will be some noise (and tough shit if you don't want it to go ahead because the DJ has been ordered and the guests have replied), but they're doing the 'neighbourly thing' and letting you know.

Sure, this approach might be okay for your neighbours, if it's only a once-off or you don't plan on living there for too long, but use this approach with your team, and you lose respect. And when they don't respect you, they're unlikely to embrace the change and actually come to the party.

Change is too often rolled out way too quickly and with way too little involvement or engagement from staff. And so often the change is shut down, like a party at midnight (when the police arrive, for the third time ...).

It takes double the effort to go back to the beginning, correct the change, make adjustments and build commitment with your staff, when, if you'd focused on the right areas at the right time, the change would have been successful the first time.

Aside from the obvious cost and effort that goes into redoing things, getting it wrong also erodes the confidence your team has with you as a leader. When you're not keeping them informed, seeking different perspectives and adapting your approach, how are you expecting to gain and retain the respect of your team?

A dynamic leader understands that to gain commitment from their people, they need to feel like they've been involved, they need to feel like they matter and they need to feel like their leader cares about their opinion.

When your team 'buy in' to an idea, they will engage and when you have the engagement of your staff you have a 'super-power'. You have a group of people who are fully committed to making things work and this trust and engagement will be part of your culture. Your team won't take time to weigh up the pros and cons; they'll back you 100 per cent because you care about perspective, you act with curiosity and you adapt to every situation to achieve the best outcome.

CHAPTER 10
INFLUENCE RESULTS

When you have invested in relationships with your team and the level of trust is high *and* when you have inspired respect and built a high level of engagement, *then* you can turn your attention to influencing results.

What we will look at in this chapter of the book builds upon what we have covered so far in the previous chapters looking at relationships and respect. This chapter focuses on how to empower your staff, how you hold them accountable and ensure you're being transparent in everything you do. How this all comes together in the Dynamic Leadership model is shown in figure 10.1.

Figure 10.1: The Dynamic Leadership model and the say, do, be of results

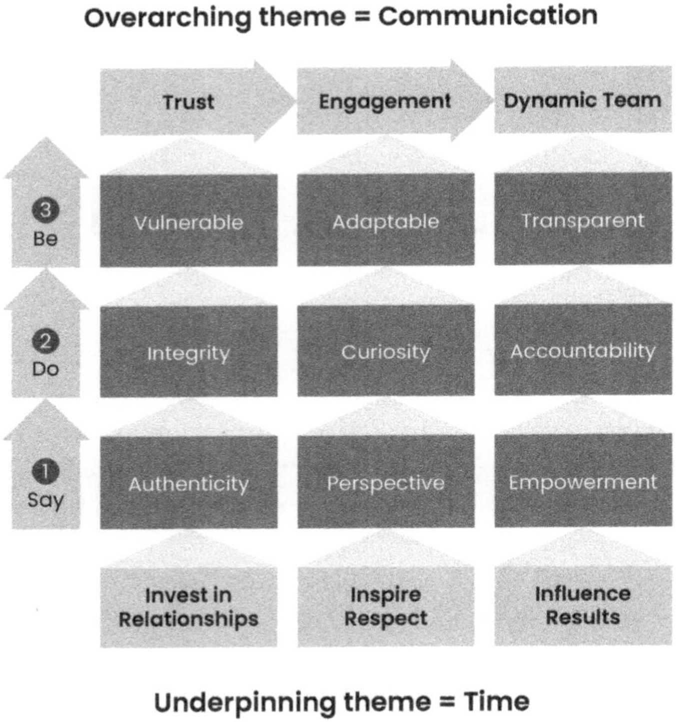

Before getting to the specific elements within results, let's firstly look at your attitude towards action versus inaction.

Inaction versus action when influencing results

If you're anything like me, results and taking action will be a very big reason for getting out of bed in the morning. Knowing that I have things to accomplish gives me energy and motivates me.

If you gave me the choice to help someone renovate their house on a weekend or sit in front of the TV and watch endless episodes of my favourite series on Netflix, I would help the person renovate their house. See, I don't like sitting still or doing nothing so my natural inclination is to 'do'. Even when I am watching TV, I will be 'doing' something else at the same time, like cooking, folding laundry or sorting through basic emails. I really struggle to stop and just 'be'!

One of my ongoing areas of development is to stop, and to give myself time to reflect, prepare, create or just ponder the possibilities. I have been working on these things but inevitably make them a task I then 'do', which kind of defeats the purpose. I will find somewhere inspiring to sit, like a park bench by the river, set the timer on my phone for 15 minutes and 'do' being present. For the first five minutes I'm looking around at the environment and noticing different things, like the colour of the water, the sounds in the trees and the movement in the grass. Then my mind will wander and I'll think about all the things I still need to achieve, and then wonder how long I've been doing nothing. Then I'll catch myself and focus on my breathing before going through the cycle again. The 15 minutes feels like two hours and when the timer goes off I feel a wave of relief that I can go back to my comfort zone of 'do'.

I could easily enough say that doing nothing just isn't my thing and leave it at that but I know it's the reason I've struggled in certain areas of my life for years. The benefit of just 'being' and reflecting has been in my blind spot and now that I know that I'm consciously incompetent at it I want to learn more. So as part of my daily ritual, I allow time for my mind to just wander. It's generally when I'm doing a task that comes automatically, like cooking or walking, but instead of listening to a podcast or watching a TV show, I will just give myself some quiet time. And I'm learning not to be hard on myself when I'm not 'doing' it the right way; I just let my mind do its own thing and notice what comes up.

It is the interest I have taken in mindfulness and slowing down my pace that has given me valuable time to think things through. If I was still focusing just on delivering results, I probably wouldn't have completed this book with the depth it has. You would quite likely be holding a very thin, 20-page book that just captured the actions you need to take, and I would be unlikely to recommend you read it.

So through all this slowing down and reflecting, I have come to realise that for leaders to deliver results, they don't necessarily have to take a lot of action. Action is definitely where many new leaders feel the most comfortable, because they feel a sense of accomplishment in the short term, but over a longer period it's not an effective way to influence your team to deliver. Your main lesson from this chapter of the book is to work out what the result actually is and whether it requires action from you, or whether it requires inaction – that is, for you to simply enable your team to do their job. Influencing results isn't controlling what others do or doing the work yourself. It's providing the right environment, support and encouragement for your staff to be their best.

When your staff know you and respect you they will assume greater responsibility for their individual performance along with the performance of the team. They will do what it takes to ensure ongoing and sustainable success. And this starts with empowerment.

Empowerment

empowerment
noun
1. Authority or power given to someone to do something.

Until you can trust your staff to make the right decisions and take the right action, you will continue to be tempted to do the work yourself. And, if you've read the book up to this point, you'll know that continuing to do the work yourself will lead to burnout and dysfunctional leadership. Empowering your staff is the only next step in successfully creating a dynamic team.

So what does empowering your staff actually mean? Let me first share with you what it is *not*. It is not:

- Giving them a task that they have never done before and expecting that they will work it out themselves without any guidance or support from you.
- Giving them a task that you continue to micromanage the activity on and control their every step and decision.
- Giving them a task with no direction and then taking it back when they haven't achieved what you expected.
- Giving them a task with vague instructions and an unclear outcome and ultimately setting them up for failure.

I hear so many leaders say something along the lines of, 'Yeah, empowerment doesn't work in my team. I tried it once and it was a disaster!' Creating an empowered team takes time to set up and ongoing support to maintain. It's not something you try once and then reject, before reverting back to the way you've always done things – this is not your way forward.

Before you can confidently empower your staff, you must have a level of trust and comfort that they can make the right decisions, even if they're different from yours. You must also believe they have the right skill level and experience to complete the task independently. Again, many leaders will give a task to their staff along with a vague description of what is required and assume they'll figure it out. What's required is an upfront investment from you to walk through how a task is performed prior to empowering them to do it on their own.

You might do the task the first time with them watching and taking notes along the way. The second time you may ask them to perform the task while you watch and provide feedback. By the third time they will be ready to complete it on their own, with your support if they need it. It's not until the third time that you'll start to save some time and feel the pressure release a little. In most situations when you're empowering your staff, it's likely to get harder before it gets easier. The key is to plan effectively and commit once you've decided to go ahead, and then see it through to the end.

When you try to cut corners and not invest the time upfront, your staff will inevitably fail – and you're likely to blame them for their incompetence rather than how well you set them up for success in the beginning. While you might be thinking, *That's a little harsh, Shelley*, I want you to know that my comments come from observation and experience with hundreds of leaders. So while it might not refer to you directly, I'm sure you'll know another leader who does this. Perhaps you could lend them your copy of the book once you've finished with it!

If you haven't 'empowered' your staff and aren't sure where to start, here are some areas to focus on, along with some questions to ask yourself to help work out whether you and your staff are ready for you to step back and allow them to take control over a task:

- *Desire:* 'Does the staff member I'm thinking about empowering have the desire to grow and develop?' Your outcome will generally be more positive if you can align it to someone's longer term career goal. They will see performing the task as a great way to get exposure to a future role and prove their ability.
- *Skill level:* 'Does the staff member have the right skill level to learn and complete the task?' This might mean having a base level of knowledge in a certain system or process that can be built upon. Does this knowledge align with a natural strength or the strong desire to improve proficiency in this area? For example, if communication isn't a natural strength of a particular staff member but they have a base level of comprehension and a strong desire to improve, they're likely going to be a great person to empower.
- *Agreement:* 'Does the staff member actually want to take on the task?' I remember when I was little watching my older sister make Mum and Dad a cup of coffee. I'm not sure how you get an instant cup of coffee so terribly wrong but my parents never asked her to do it again. I can only conclude that she didn't want to do it so she purposely did it so wrong that she would never have to do it again. If you think this might be the case with a certain staff member, you may choose to pick someone else. Another option is simply being prepared for the staff member to fail the first time before getting them to do it again. This behaviour doesn't tend to continue when they know the task is going to stay with them until

it's done correctly, so sometimes it's just a matter of seeing it through to completion.

- *Letting go:* 'Am I ready to let go of "my way" of doing things?' Sometimes we need to have a firm word with ourselves and get over needing to be in control of everything all the time. For me, this is still something I struggle with but I'm aware of it and so I can usually catch myself in the moment and 'let it go'.
- *Outcome:* 'Do I know what I want the outcome to be? What's the purpose of doing this task?' It's surprising how often we ask our staff to do a task that is vague and ambiguous – and one where not even we know what the outcome is going to be. For other tasks, leaders can simply assume both they and the staff member want the same outcome, but the leader hasn't clearly defined what that is. So where possible, define the outcome you expect from the task, specifically. If you don't know the outcome for a task, consider whether delegating it to a staff member is appropriate. If you want their creative input, the outcome might simply be getting them to brainstorm some ideas and then coming back together to determine next steps.
- *Rules of engagement:* 'Have I communicated to my staff about when I want the task completed? Do they know how/when/what I would like them to keep me informed along the way?' This one isn't as common but I have seen leaders get frustrated with staff who agree to take on a task and then provide no progress updates, just radio silence. They don't know they should be keeping their leader updated and the leader tends to come to all sorts of incorrect conclusions about what's going on with

them. So establishing how you want to be engaged from the beginning will avoid a lot of angst along the way.

- *Decision-making powers:* 'Does the staff member know what they can make decisions on and what needs to be referred up?' Empowering staff doesn't mean you need to hand over whole processes or functions; instead, you may only want to empower them to make decisions up to a certain level and then refer decisions to you. Or you might want to be part of a particular decision if it's highly sensitive. Again, you can't assume that they will know when to involve you so give further detail around this where possible. If you don't tell them, you can't blame them when things go wrong.
- *The teaching process:* 'Have I taught the staff member how to perform the task and watched them do it at least once on their own?' As already mentioned, the staff member will likely not be able to complete the task by themselves until at least the third time doing it.
- *Support:* 'Does the staff member have the necessary support throughout performing the task? Will I be available if they have questions or need clarification?' If you're not going to be available, find someone who will help them if they need it. It's important that staff feel like they're supported and not abandoned.

Once you've set the right environment to empower your staff, it's time for you to get out of their way. Leave them to get on with the task and trust they'll do the best they can with the resources they have. Believe in their ability to give the task the right level of attention and represent you as best they can. Finally, if the task they've been given doesn't go to plan, never ever throw them under the bus. Take the responsibility for what has happened and talk to them about it.

With effective empowerment comes a really strong feedback loop. If certain things were done really well, share it. Similarly, if certain things could be done better in the future, take the time to reflect with the staff member and learn from mistakes.

Adopt a mindset of 'there is no failure, only feedback' and each time you empower your staff they'll be better than the last time.

Remember – empowering your staff is a process that takes time to set up but gets quicker and easier over time and is well worth the investment. By empowering your staff, you will build their confidence, their skillset and their motivation. More importantly, you will have more time to work on the things that matter most and allow you to evolve as a leader.

Accountability

accountable
adjective
1. Required or expected to justify actions or decisions; responsible.
2. Able to be explained or understood.

Accountability is kind of like the glue that holds everything together. It's a way to calibrate what is being said and done and make adjustments where necessary. A leader who cannot hold their staff accountable will fail to hold the respect of their team over time.

Many leaders, particularly in smaller businesses, expect the staff member they've recently hired to just go ahead and do what they're supposed to do without so much as a proper conversation. And it's nice to know that some people actually will jump straight in and give it a go, but they are the exception not the rule. Most people like to know what's expected and then they like to know that there's some type of reward for getting it right or some type of consequence for getting it wrong or not doing it at all.

Real-life example

I remember speaking with the owner of a hair salon who just couldn't find good stylists. There was always a problem with their performance and so their turnover was higher than average. When I asked her what the process was to induct and train a new stylist to the salon, she said, 'I show them around so they know where all the equipment is and teach them the booking system [which was a paper notebook that sat at the front counter] and then I let them get on with it.' No conversation about the business's values, how they differentiate from other salons, how they take their clients through the process, nothing.

I then asked her about what happens when they're not doing things the way she wanted them done. She said, 'Oh, I just cut their shifts back until they eventually leave', without a single conversation about what they were doing wrong. When I asked if she ever gave any type of feedback she said, 'No. If they're a qualified stylist, they should already know these things; it's common knowledge, it's what we all do.'

What I took from the conversation was this: for stylists to have a long career working in this salon they needed to be able to read minds and anticipate what the owner liked and didn't like! That's not too much to expect, surely?!

While this particular business owner was at the extreme end of avoiding conflict, she's not alone in her approach to conversations. How often have you said to yourself, 'I'll let that go; I'm sure they didn't mean it' or 'I won't say anything this time; I'm sure it's just a "one-off"'? Do you expect behaviour will autocorrect? Sometimes it might, but it's rare. Often the behaviour will continue, and can even get worse over time if nothing is said.

Hold yourself accountable!

So why aren't you having the hard conversations? The most popular response I hear is, 'I don't want to upset anyone' followed by 'they're still quite new' and then 'I'm sure they didn't mean it' … and so on and so on. We find ways to justify why we haven't had the conversation and reassure ourselves that we'll do it next time … and then we don't, but we have different reasons – so the cycle continues.

As well as not wanting to confront someone, however, perhaps you're also avoiding accountability conversations because you're afraid of being labelled a hypocrite. In other words, you're not following through on your own commitments, so you can't very well challenge your staff on their shortcomings. Perhaps you do one of these things:

- Offer to do things for your staff that you know aren't a priority and will never get done.
- Agree to unrealistic timeframes and don't say they're unachievable until after the due date has passed.
- Regularly make commitments and then forget about them.
- Say yes to doing tasks you know nothing about and set them aside hoping they're never mentioned again.

- Commit to connecting staff with people in your network who can assist with their professional development, but then get busy, deprioritise it and make excuses for why you haven't followed through.

If you are guilty of doing any of these things, having 'accountability conversations' with your staff is a waste of time and you will be seen as a hypocrite. Your staff will assume you don't respect them and the conversation won't change their behaviour. You're just likely to end up with a team who are disengaged and potentially resentful.

When you share your actions or intentions with others, you open yourself up to be challenged on the outcome. This verbalisation in itself generally motivates people to fulfil the task and avoid being challenged.

For those of you who need some more motivation, or perhaps suffer from procrastination or a lack of follow-through, consider some of the following strategies to hold yourself accountable:

- Find an accountability partner to check in with on a regular basis and keep you on track. Make sure they do not tolerate excuses and challenge you when they feel you've lost focus.
- Make your commitment public by sharing your agreed actions and timeline with others. You could put it on social media or tell a friend or colleague.
- Make it visual by creating a vision board or setting a reminder on your phone to monitor progress.
- Create a checklist to break down your tasks into smaller activities and check them off as they're completed.

For further tips in this area, refer to chapter 6.

If you still miss a commitment (which can happen on the rare occasion), continue to hold yourself accountable to your staff. Talk to them about what happened and what you're going to do to avoid it happening in the future and then make sure you follow through.

If you're doing what you say you're going to do (in other words, acting with integrity), becoming comfortable with 'accountability conversations' is simple, but you do have to keep certain aspects in mind.

The following sections outline the steps I recommend you follow to easily hold your team accountable.

Set expectations

Make sure both you and your staff are clear on what the expected objectives or outcomes of the task are from the very beginning. If you haven't set expectations, you can't give feedback on something you just 'assume' they should know. As mentioned in the empowerment section, setting expectations includes outlining the desired outcome and the rules of engagement, and being aware of the teaching process. If you've forgotten to share information with them at the start of the task, any feedback at the end of the process is simply a note for next time. It won't be an accountability conversation.

Agree on a time frame for delivery

When you ask your staff to perform a task, you absolutely must give them a time frame to complete it within. Without a time frame, nothing is ever 'not done' – it's simply 'not done yet'. So let them know when you would like the task to be complete and then ask whether that time frame fits into their schedule. The conversation here might expand to other priorities and making a decision around what should be done first and this is perfectly okay. As long as both parties agree that the final time frame is acceptable and achievable.

Remember – you are responsible for observing non-verbal cues with your staff when setting time frames. Often staff will agree to the time frame you've suggested because you're 'the boss', even if it's not realistic. In these instances, you will likely see their physiology (body language) doesn't match what they're saying, so you'll need to ask them further questions to get them to open up. You might ask something like, 'What other things are you working on right now that might need to be put on hold?', 'If you commit to completing this task by the agreed time, what isn't going to get done?' or 'Can you achieve this time frame without working extra hours?' Get them to open up about what's going on with their workload and adjust the time frame or other priorities to make sure they can achieve what you're setting out.

The other thing to note around gaining agreement on time frames is that if it isn't a solid 'yes' then it's a 'no'. Agreement doesn't come with, 'Yeah, that should be okay' or 'I'll try' or 'Okay, I'll see what I can do', it needs to be definite. You may think this is a small thing but I promise you it can be the thing that makes all the difference.

Finally, once the time frame is agreed, ask if they need support with anything to ensure it's met.

Openly discuss consequences

This step isn't required in every instance but is absolutely essential if your staff member has failed to meet your expectations in the past. Ask them what 'might' happen if they miss this deadline. This could be focused around what 'might' happen to the business or the team or you as their leader and then their colleagues. Once you're comfortable they understand the flow-on impacts of not doing what they've just committed to, ask them what the consequence might be for them personally.

Ask the staff member to come up with all possible consequences – for example:

- 'I'll have to stay back after hours to complete it.'
- 'It will reflect on my monthly performance results.'
- 'I will be put on to a performance improvement plan.' (This might apply if the issue is ongoing.)
- 'We will have another conversation.' (This can often be all that is needed.)
- 'I will lose my job.'
- 'I will buy coffees for the whole team.'
- 'I will attend the next senior leadership meeting.'

You get the idea. It doesn't really matter what the consequence is as long as it's enough to give them the motivation they need to follow through on their commitment.

Of course, if they fail to follow through on their commitment, you need the next section …

Have an accountability conversation

If the objective or outcome isn't achieved or the due date is missed, an 'accountability conversation' should be held. The conversation will start with you restating what was agreed in the initial discussion. Some questions you might like to ask to get the conversation going include:

- How are you doing?
- Is everything okay?

- I'm just checking-in on the task I gave you. You agreed to finishing it by the 3rd and it's now the 5th, so I'm wondering what happened? (Give your staff member enough silence to come up with their own response: *do not* respond on their behalf.)
- Okay, do you remember what you agreed the consequences would be?

The following sections offer some tips on how to follow these questions.

Let them come to their own conclusion

Generally, if you've given them a period of silence to reflect, staff will either concede their mistake and accept the consequences, or they might try to give excuses (which you'll softly challenge). It's important to make the conversation as open and supportive as possible. The key intention for having this conversation is to get your staff to come to their own realisations about how they approached the task.

Take the lessons

Once they've started to offer some insights and conclusions, say, 'Okay, great. So what might you do next time?' Help them to adopt new thought patterns, behaviours and ways of working. These might include prioritisation of work or realising that they don't have the capacity or skillset to complete the task. So your focus then could be on minimising distractions or perhaps providing additional training and support.

Offer support

Finally, ask them if you can do anything to support them through this change. Again, it's important that you wait until they've come to their own conclusions before you offer support, or they may transfer the responsibility over to you. If they do need support from you, make sure you follow through on anything you commit to.

Repeat!

If you're having 'accountability conversations' regularly, your staff will learn very quickly to manage expectations better. Your conversations will become less frequent and your team will become more engaged and productive.

Remember that the behaviour you accept will continue. It is up to you to first be a role model with your own behaviour and then hold your staff accountable for theirs.

What's in a word?

An extension of accountability is the words you use in your conversations. If you have staff who aren't following through or doing what is expected, you may want to consider what language you're using in your discussions.

Sometimes the language you use can unintentionally dilute or distort the message you're communicating. Here are three words that, when used in the wrong context, can affect accountability in your team:

1. *But:* This word should rarely be used. In fact, as a general rule you should stop saying it completely. 'But' discounts what you've just said and can undermine your authenticity as a leader. For example, 'You're doing a great job, but some improvements need to be made.' Instead, simply use the word 'and'.
2. *Try:* This word is annoying! As Yoda from *Star Wars* says, 'Do. Or do not. There is no try.' 'Try' is non-committal

and can come across as not being invested in the person or outcome. For example, 'I'll try to get this done by the end of the week.' Instead, use the word 'will' – or 'won't' if you're not realistically going to have the time.

3. *We:* This word should be used to create a sense of belonging and, in the right context, is very effective. Be careful not to use 'we' when you're managing the performance of an individual, however. In this context, 'we' can provide the perfect opportunity for underperformers to avoid taking responsibility. For example, 'What can we do to improve your performance?', to which the staff member might put the responsibility back on you as their leader. Instead, use the words 'you' and 'I'. For example, 'What can you do to improve your performance? This is what I will commit to doing.'

If you're struggling to move your team into action, looking at your word choice might be part of your solution. Remember that sometimes it's the smallest changes that can have the largest impacts.

Have the conversation!

Holding your staff accountable doesn't have to be a challenging conversation. The reason these conversations become challenging is because we put off having them until we're totally pissed off with a person's actions or behaviours – so we have to manage not only the content of the conversation but also the emotions that have built up over time.

Never have an accountability conversation when you're already frustrated or annoyed with someone. Let the emotions pass and go into the conversation with openness, curiosity and patience to let your staff member work through their own thought processes.

Remember that conversations you avoid bubble away under the surface and do real damage to trust and the strength and resilience of a relationship over time. Susan Scott, author of *Fierce Conversations*, sums this up perfectly:

> *The conversation is the relationship. If the conversation stops, all of the possibilities for the relationship become smaller and all of the possibilities for the individuals in the relationship become smaller, until one day we overhear ourselves in mid-sentence, making ourselves smaller in every encounter, behaving as if we are just the space around our shoes, engaged in yet another three-minute conversation so empty of meaning it crackles.*

Transparent

> **transparent**
> *adjective*
> 1. (of a material or article) allowing light to pass through so that objects behind can be distinctly seen.
> 2. Easy to perceive or detect.
> 2.1 Having thoughts or feelings that are easily perceived; open.
> 2.2 (of an organisation or its activities) open to public scrutiny.

The final component of the Dynamic Leadership model and this book is to be transparent. If you've worked your way through the model and the book, you are now investing in relationships and developing a deeper level of trust with your staff, and you are inspiring respect and encouraging healthy conflict. You are empowering your staff to take control and you're holding both them and yourself accountable. Transparency is really just the cherry on top of a deliciously constructed cake.

Transparency is often shown as a core business value or customer promise, and rightfully so. Both customers and staff want to believe they're seeing the full picture or hearing the full story. Seasoned leaders may have worked on being fully transparent for a number of years but, as a new leader, perhaps you sometimes find knowing what to share with your team and what to withhold a little difficult.

Being transparent doesn't mean telling everyone about everything – no doubt you can think of certain things you must not share with your staff, and nor would your staff expect you to. Transparency isn't about full disclosure; it's about being open to disclose what can be disclosed and, at the same time, being honest and completely unapologetic about what must stay confidential.

Real-life example

I once worked for a leader who did transparency so well! He would say to his leadership team, 'There are things I can share with you and there are things I can't share. I'm not going to promise to tell you everything. What I can promise is that I will share as much as I can with you so that you understand what's happening at a higher level and feel like you're equipped to make the right decisions with your team.' And he followed through on his promise. We never felt like he was being deceptive and trusted that he was sharing what he could and doing the right thing by his people.

During the time I worked for him, the organisation went through several restructures, and each time we knew they were coming and we had a reasonable idea of how we might be affected. This gave us the opportunity to prepare our teams for change and think about what might be next. His was one of the few teams with engagement scores that increased, even despite the restructure and loss of roles for some people.

Don't be lazy

So why do some leaders lack transparency? I have a theory that only two types of leaders lack transparency: the narcissistic leader and the lazy leader.

If you're still reading the book at this point, I'm going to assume you're not a narcissistic leader who holds other people back for your own personal gain. This type of leader doesn't want anyone to be better than them and deliberately withholds information to keep their staff dependent on them.

The lazy leader, on the other hand, finds the sharing of information all too hard and is too lazy to work out what to communicate and what to withhold, so they withhold everything. They generally don't realise the damage they do by not communicating effectively with their team. Staff are frequently taken by surprise and over time this type of leader will lose credibility and the confidence of their team.

If you are going to empower your team to make the right decisions, you need to be giving them all of the information they need to make these decisions. When you're doing this, you're operating with full transparency and your team will operate in the same way. When your team culture embraces transparency, no necessary conversation will be left unsaid, no idea will be held back for fear of how others may perceive it, and no dream will be too unrealistic for staff to want to share with you.

One of the best signs that you are operating with full transparency is when a staff member can come to you and say, 'I don't think my career is with this organisation anymore; I need help to move on' and you can give them your full support, without judgement and without your opinion. You will also be completely transparent about the opportunity this will present to redefine their role and improve it for the next person and seek their support to make it happen.

Avoiding misinformation and opinion

If I think about the impact that transparency has on customer experience, I automatically gravitate to product recalls and how they are managed with the public. In the past, product recalls were dealt with quickly and quietly; they were covered up or brushed under the carpet so as not to tarnish the brand. Today, businesses are open to sharing faults with products. Organisations now realise that customers don't want perfect, they want honest. Most customers will forgive a defect or recall if the brand concedes they made a mistake – and if the brand then does what they need to do to rectify the mistake so the inconvenience to customers is minimised. Customers will usually forgive honest mistakes. Not only this, but the more transparent a business is, the more trust is built, and a stronger relationship is created.

When a mistake is downplayed, diluted or hidden completely, trust will erode. So now when a product recall occurs, businesses are very quick to let the public know about what is going on. They will share how it happened and, most importantly, how they are going about fixing the current issue. They will also share their lessons learnt and the changes they're making to prevent future occurrences. When dealt with in this way, customers generally don't see recalls as being a huge issue and are likely to continue doing business with that brand or product. It works the same way for leaders – only your customers are your staff.

The other benefit to being fully transparent is that gossip and the good old rumour mill have no place. When you are operating with full transparency, your staff have less to make assumptions around. If you are not being transparent, your staff will quickly work to fill in the gaps – and I can guarantee their imagination and what they come up with is a whole lot more creative than the reality of the situation. When you give enough information for your staff to feel safe and informed, these conversations become null and void.

Transparency is being open about whatever you can be without giving your opinion. Opinions don't need to be disclosed – in fact, they should not actually be offered unless someone asks for them. Your opinion is the conclusion you've made about various pieces of information. This conclusion may be correct, but it is more likely just to be one of many different ways of looking at a situation. So the more you can stick to fact and concrete information, the better able your staff will be to form their own opinions, without your bias included.

Celebrating success and integrity

Operating from a position of transparency allows you to celebrate individual successes as well as overall team performance. It also allows you to critically analyse processes when things didn't go as planned and identify what needs to be done in future. When I think about teams that operate with high success, and are effective in a sustainable way, transparency is always high on their list of priorities.

If you are unsure whether information can be shared with your team, then ask. Make a point, in every meeting that you attend, to ask for confidentiality requirements. 'Is there anything that is being discussed in this meeting that I cannot share with my team?' Or, if you already know the meeting has a high level of sensitivity, you may ask, 'Is there anything in this meeting that I can disclose to my team?' Gain the approval of the meeting host to share the information, always ensuring you maintain your own integrity and are being transparent with your intentions for the information you are gathering.

Transparency aligns really well with integrity. It's important for you as a leader, regardless of the relationship that you have with a person, to never ever disclose information that you are not authorised to disclose. If you compromise your integrity around this just once, your staff will always question whether they can trust you. To add to that, if you need to talk to someone about information you've received that is highly confidential, consider talking to a qualified coach. A coach holds privacy and confidentiality at the centre of everything that they do, so whatever takes place with a client remains between the coach and the client. Sometimes having a conversation about something that's bothering you with a coach can help you work through your own thoughts and figure out the best action to take.

Remember – share what you can, don't share what you can't and always ask permission if the information is not yours to use.

CONCLUSION

Congratulations! If you've read all the chapters in this book, you've made your way through all the components of the Dynamic Leadership model (repeated again here in case you need to jog your memory).

The Dynamic Leadership model

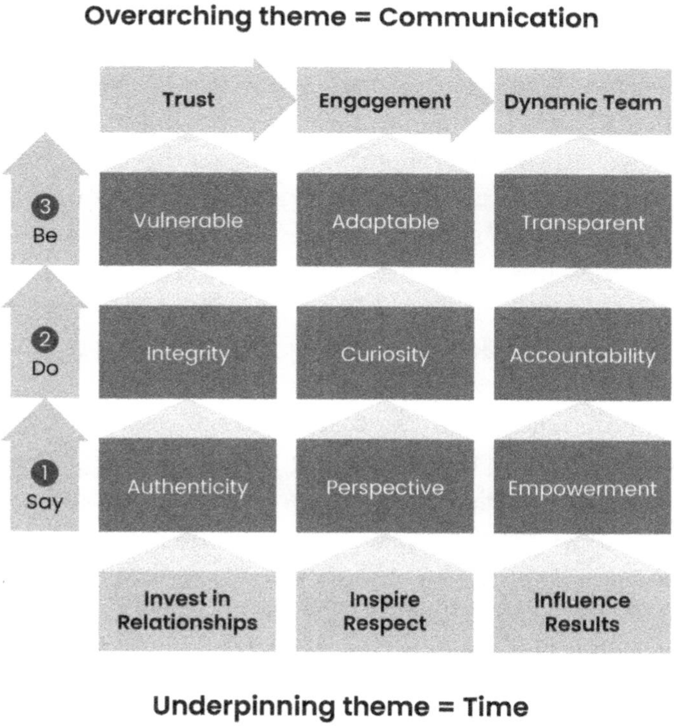

Having taught the concepts in this book in training over the past few years, the content I included came to me very naturally – and I'm actually a little sad it's come to an end. I'm hoping the topics I've written about and the model I've shared are easy for you to relate to. I haven't shared anything revolutionary; that was not my intention. My intention was to equip you with a guide to improve your focus and do the things that make the difference. I have pulled all the components I see as being essential to a new leader's success and ordered them in a way that makes sense and follows a logical pathway.

My intention was also to share my own journey of leadership, highlighting where I got things terribly wrong and where I made things so wonderfully right. If I can offer a different perspective, I know it will make a difference. My one hope for all leaders is for them to avoid ever having to go through what I went through. Hopefully, by reading this book, you can learn from my mistakes and get it right the first time around.

I have realised that the greatest rewards are those that come from enormous challenges. I have felt more emotion since becoming a leader than in any other area of my life (including becoming a mother, although they're closely related). I have never cried so much, fought with so much conviction, felt so frustrated, laughed so hard and cared so deeply than in my role of leading people. My biggest realisation is that people matter and, without the dedication and support of its people, a business will simply fail to exist. The other realisation is that it's okay to think differently – it's okay not to agree, and it's even okay to have the occasional tantrum because you are human and that's what makes you awesome! Life isn't about getting others to conform to one way of doing things; life is about learning to adapt, understand and appreciate everyone's differences, and appreciate the excitement and diversity that comes with it.

I want to leave you with a final thought, on what I think you're truly capable of. As a 'C' average student right through school, I didn't believe I was capable of doing much more with my life than working in a factory or in a restaurant as a waitress. I listened to way too many people who gave their opinion on what I could do with my life. I ruled out ever becoming a doctor or a lawyer and I even ruled out ever working in a bank – which is where I spent a decade of my career. I believed people when they would say things like, 'If you're not good at this, you'll never be able to do that.'

I believe you are capable of doing anything! If you want something badly enough and if you're prepared to get a little dirty and feel a little uncomfortable along the way, what you want you can have! If you're drinking the 'comfortable and safe' Kool-Aid and it's starting to taste a little sour, I think it's time to swap drinks.

Stop listening to people who want to protect you and keep you safe and start listening to people who will tell you what you need to hear and push you to learn and grow and become the best version of yourself.

A great example of what people are capable of is the story of the first 4-minute mile. In the early 1950s, the world record for the fastest mile run was set at 4:01minutes, which had remained unbeaten for over a decade. The belief was that it wasn't humanly possible to run a mile in under 4 minutes. That was until Roger Bannister, a 25-year-old medical student, had a theory that this limit could be broken … and on 6 May 1954 he did exactly that, running the mile in 3:59.4! In training, he had changed his focus to physiology and running 'consistent' laps, which reduced the consumption of oxygen required, and this changed the result. He broke the mile into quarters and focused on running consistent quarter-mile laps. This meant each lap needed to be run in under 1 minute, and this consumed his attention. When he finished in under 4 minutes, he broke not only the track record in Oxford (where the run took place) but also the British, European, Commonwealth and World Record at the same time.

The best part about this story is that once the myth had been busted on what was 'humanly possible', Bannister's time was broken just 46 days later by Australian John Landy, who ran the mile in 3:57.9.

Over the last 60 years, 1,300 men have broken the 4-minute barrier and the current world record, held by Moroccan Hicham El Guerrouj, sits at 3:43. (No women have yet broken the 4-minute barrier, with the current record set at 4:12.56, but watch this space!)

If you can shift your focus to what you believe is possible, you can become whoever you want to be, regardless of what other people tell you!

Thanks so much for taking the time to read this book. This is by no means the end of your leadership development; it is just the beginning. This is the place where leadership begins, and where leaders learn to follow the right leader and become the leader their staff are willing to follow.

Be kind, be your best and pay it forward!

Shelley
shelleyflett.com

PAY IT FORWARD

Now that you've finished this book, you may want to read it all over again! Or you may want to keep it for a while, dipping into certain areas as needed for a quick refresher or more significant rework. Use it as you see fit. Once you've got what you need from this book, however, please pass it on to someone else. My biggest mantra in life is to 'pay it forward'. If we can all help two or three or four people to succeed, the world's bound to become a better place. When we can give to others without expecting anything in return, we've reached the pinnacle of what it means to be a true leader. Knowing that my book is helping to improve culture and results is success to me so keep the book moving – and feel free to add your own words of wisdom as you pass it along.

As a leader, you have your own unique experience, and this could make a difference to someone else. However, we're not always good at sharing our lessons with others. My own story, which I share through the book, is definitely not one I'm proud of. For a long time I was too embarrassed to share it with anyone – I wanted it hidden, buried and concreted over so no-one ever found out. But as my ego repaired and my confidence resurfaced, I knew this wasn't something to keep to myself. As I began to share my story, I found many people had stories similar to my own, and these people were equally ashamed and punishing themselves unnecessarily.

It's time to get real! Share your story and tell the next reader how you've failed and what you learnt along the way.

Let's make the leadership playground safe enough to fall and get back up again.

Pay it forward

As I pass this book onto the next reader, I'd like to share a little about my own lessons as a leader:

Name:______________________________ Date:______________

My story:____

____

____

____

____

____

____

Name:______________________________ Date:______________

My story:____

____

____

____

____

____

____

Name:________________ Date:________

My story:____________________

Name:________________ Date:________

My story:____________________

Name:________________ Date:________

My story:____________________

Name:______________________________ Date:______________

My story:____

Name:______________________________ Date:______________

My story:____

Name:______________________________ Date:______________

My story:____

SOURCES

Chapter 1

Prosci. (2019) 'People, Change, Results' framework, January 2019, https://www.prosci.com

Victorian Department of Education. (2018) 'Summary Statistics for Victorian Schools: July 2018', https://www.education.vic.gov.au/Documents/about/department/brochurejuly.pdf

University Rankings. (2019), 'Australian University Student Numbers', Accessed January 2019, http://www.universityrankings.com.au/university-student-numbers.html

Chapter 2

Hubbard, T. (2016) 'Research: Delegating More Can Increase Your Earnings', *Harvard Business Review*, https://hbr.org/2016/08/research-delegating-more-can-increase-your-earnings

Scott, S. (2002) *Fierce Conversations: Achieving success in work and in life, one conversation at a time*, Piatkus Books

Chapter 4

Barnes, M. 'Project Management with the Time, Cost, Quality Triangle: Is it still the best way?', Distant Production House University, http://www.dphu.org/uploads/attachements/books/books_5676_0.pdf

Curtiss, P. and Warren, P. (1973) *The Dynamics of Life Skills Coaching*, Prince Albert, Sask

Kegan, R. & Laskov Lahey, L. (2009) *Immunity to Change*, Harvard Business Review Press

Chapter 5

Luntz, F. (2008) *Words That Work: It's Not What You Say, It's What People Hear*, Hyperion

Mehrabian, A. (1981) *Silent messages: Implicit communication of emotions and attitudes.* Belmont, CA: Wadsworth (currently distributed by Albert Mehrabian)

Chapter 6

Cirillo, F. (2018) *The Pomodoro Technique: Life-Changing Time-Management System*, Ebury Publishing

Kruse, K. (2016) 'The 80/20 Rule and How It Can Change Your Life', *Forbes*, https://www.forbes.com/sites/kevinkruse/2016/03/07/80-20-rule/#2b0176af3814

Pink, D. (2011) *Drive: The surprising truth about what motivates us*, Riverhead Books

Tracy, B. (2013) *Eat That Frog! Get More of the Important Things Done – Today!*, Hodder & Stoughton General Division

Chapter 8

Bell, P. (2017) 'The History of Friendship: How Friendship Evolved and Why It's Fundamental To Your Happiness', *Huffington Post*, https://www.huffingtonpost.co.uk/2014/02/10/history-of-friendship-evolution_n_4743572.html

James, T. & Woodsmall, W. (2017) *Time Line Therapy and the Basis of Personality: Pedagogy for a Changing World*, Crown House Publishing

Lencioni, P. (2002) *The Five Dysfunctions of a Team: A Leadership Fable*, John Wiley & Sons Inc.

McLeod, S. (2018) 'Solomon Asch – Conformity Experiment', *Simply Psychology*, https://www.simplypsychology.org/asch-conformity.html

Tracy, B. (2018) 'The Importance of Honesty and Integrity in Business', Brian Tracy International, https://www.briantracy.com/blog/leadership-success/importance-of-honesty-integrity-in-business/

Chapter 9

Goleman, D. (2017) *Leadership That Gets Results* (Harvard Business Review Classics), Harvard Business Review Press

Lewis, B. (2012), *Magic of NLP Demystified*, Second Edition, Crown House Publishing

Napell, S.M. (1976) 'Six Common Non-Facilitating Teaching Behaviors', *Contemporary Education*: 47, 2, 79–82, Winter 76, http://ecommons.med.harvard.edu/ec_res/nt/0A6821C6-76D4-400B-AA3D-E081994789F1/6_common_non-facilitating_teaching_behaviors.pdf

Sutherland, R. (2011) 'Perspective is everything', TED.com, https://www.ted.com/talks/rory_sutherland_perspective_is_everything

Wiseman, L., Allen, L & Foster, E. (2013) *The Multiplier Effect: Tapping the Genius inside Our Schools*, SAGE Publications Inc.

Chapter 10

Scott, S. (2002) *Fierce Conversations: Achieving success in work and in life, one conversation at a time*, Piatkus Books

WORK WITH SHELLEY

If you'd like to know how Shelley can work with you to transform you into a dynamic leader, through coaching, training or facilitating, please contact her on:

Email: Shelley@shelleyflett.com

Website: Shelleyflett.com

LinkedIn: www.linkedin.com/in/shelleyflett/

Facebook: www.facebook.com/Shelley-Flett-Business-Leadership-Coach-Trainer-2225335784419556

Feedback and reviews

Below are some comments on Shelley's Dynamic Leader program:

The tutelage was a very productive use of my time to help me focus more on my business, reflecting on what's important and what purpose it serves me.

Craig Brown, Bank Manager, Westpac

One of the very best sessions I have been to. Informative, simple but super effective.

Ryan Gustofson, Team Leader, Brisbane City Council

An energetic presentation, full of insights and moral humility. Thank you!

Sean Melville, Leader, Department of Transport and Main Roads

Thank you for sharing your wealth of knowledge. Appreciate your training day and I can't wait to try some techniques you've helped me develop as a new leader.
Jim Lindsay, Leader, Qld Urban Utilities

It was a great reminder of my areas of focus, such as letting them talk.
Matthew Rankin, Team Leader, City of Gold Coast

Great information and insights on how to improve myself and my team, which will allow me to take back to my whole workplace.
Gregory Wynne, Leader, Smart Service Qld

Your leadership style is relatable. Simple yet effective tips and tools. I can't wait to implement back in the office.
Bec Liddy, Leader, TAFE Qld

Very informative tutelage; this will assist with my leadership skills in the future. Very engaging and current in today's workplace. Well worth it.
Deborah Ferguson, Team Leader, QLeave

Certainly enjoyed being put on the course. I found it helpful to cover a wide range of topics. I'm looking forward to implementing some ideas and feel some of the skills learned today will take me to the next step in my business leadership journey.
Josh Ellis, Owner, Sharpline Electrics

Shelley, thank you for opening my mind, for reminding me there is always more room to personally develop. I will take and implement your teachings today to my life.
Brooke De Silva, Office Manager, L&D Picturesque Painting

Thank you for providing such inspirational insights. I can already notice a change in mindset.

Anshu Bhatiani, Manager, ANZ

Fantastic, inspiring day, well worth time away from the business. Engaging, relevant content presented in a collaborative way.

Tamara Annesley, Business Leader, Corporate Traveller, Flight Centre Group

I found today so inspiring! Makes me want to get back to the office and start trying all the learnt strategies.

Rachael Vandenberg, HR Manager, Hero360

Thoroughly interesting and focused seminar. A great worthwhile experience that I was glad to get the opportunity to partake in.

Jemimah Bradbrook, Coordinator/Shift Leader, VisionStream

I appreciated your insights into building genuine relationships. I have also been told in the past not to be 'mates' with colleagues, but I like your perspective.

Tim Kercheval, Reliability Engineer, VisionStream

There was a lot of information that I have seen before. However, I have never had it explained in a way I understood and can utilise.

James Roberts, Practice Support Analyst, MYOB

Opens the mind to explore different leadership styles for different employees.

Jamie Oxley, Territory Sales Manager, MYOB

An interesting day considering the current climate of my workforce. I found the Do, Say, Be, and Relationships, Respect, Results to be very insightful in regards to the rest of my workforce and overall health and morale of team. Thought it was great. The mobility exercises were excellent. Great day. Thanks!

Helen Grose, Operations Manager, Social Research Centre

Thanks for the workshop, Shelley. It provided me with a chance to step back and evaluate some of the practices in my office and workplace in a critical and reflexive environment. The fascia exercises were great.

Steve Pukallas, Operations Manager, Social Research Centre

The course has been so valuable for me to have the right mindset going into my leadership role. Thank you!

Candice Bosher, Business Development Manager, Corporate Traveller, Flight Centre Group

Fantastically organised and structured session that not only incorporates prior knowledge about leadership but also challenges you to look outside what you know and challenge the status quo.

Hesh Gunatillake, Manager, ANZ

The session was great! I really enjoyed Shelley's real-life examples, which made it more relatable and seem more authentic.

Sean MacLeod-Jones, Team Leader, Teachers Mutual Bank

I really enjoyed Shelley's facilitating style. It was extremely engaging and her knowledge is very clearly from experience. Thank you!

Aoife Kearns, Team Leader, Sydney Water

This experience has changed the way I approach work within my team, making it worthwhile.

Jason Frey, Customer Experience Manager, Flow Systems

Well-structured session. Thought provoking. Gained insight of the DISC model. Great speaker with great stories which people could relate to.

Rupal Patel, Manager, Family Court

The day was extremely informative providing plenty of tools I can take away to use. Shelley was fun, knowledgeable and made this a great experience.

Rachel Harris, Team Leader, Sydney Water

I loved every minute of today. It was light, interactive but very informative. You were very easy to listen to. I have only been in my role for one month so I can't wait to put these skills to use.

Jennie Wood, Manager, Auto Guru

Very interesting and interactive. I will be working on using the information I have learnt today to change the way I work as a leader.

Jenn Irving, Customer Value Leader, Suncorp Group

I love the way you hold the room and speak in front of a crowd. I was thoroughly invested all day – thank you.

Julia Shields, Team Leader, RemServ

This course allows you to do a self-assessment and provides ideas and strategies that you can use to enhance leadership skills.

Bernadette Nagy, Dispute Resolution Officer, Unity Water

Shelley was engaging throughout the course. Very inspirational. Listen and ask exercise was engaging.

Judy Matley, Team Leader, TMR

Thank you so much for today. You are very inspirational. The session was very interactive which helps avoid boredom or death by PowerPoint. Thank you for the fun and giving me some tools to help me on my way.

Rose Lewis, Leader, Sunsuper

INDEX